Blue-Tongued Skinks

By David C. Wareham

Blue-Tongued Skinks

CompanionHouse Books™ is an imprint of Fox Chapel Publishing.

Project Team
Editorial Director: Kerry Bogert
Editor: Amy Deputato
Design: Mary Ann Kahn

Dedication: To Nathan

ISBN 978-1-882770-99-1

The Cataloging-in-Publication Data is on file with the Library of Congress.

This book has been published with the intent to provide accurate and authoritative information in regard to the subject matter within. While every precaution has been taken in the preparation of this book, the author and publisher expressly disclaim any responsibility for any errors, omissions, or adverse effects arising from the use or application of the information contained herein. The techniques and suggestions are used at the reader's discretion and are not to be considered a substitute for veterinary care. If you suspect a medical problem, consult your veterinarian.

 Fox Chapel Publishing
903 Square Street
Mount Joy, PA 17552

https://www.facebook.com/companionhousebooks

We are always looking for talented authors. To submit an idea, please send a brief inquiry to acquisitions@foxchapelpublishing.com.

Printed in the United States

Contents

Introduction

At one time almost completely ignored by lizard keepers, blue-tongued skinks (part of the genus *Tiliqua*), with their distinctive berry-blue tongues, have become extremely popular. While most blue-tongued species exhibit a certain amount of variability in both pattern and color, those with greater variability—the Eastern (*T. s. scincoides*) and Blotched (*T. nigrolutea*), for example—can fetch exceptionally high prices whenever they become available.

Today, members of the blue-tongue family are generally considered the most popular, intelligent, and undemanding of pet lizards. Because they are slow moving (due to their short limbs), quickly tamed, and trustworthy in the presence of children, blue-tongued skinks are suitable for even first-time lizard keepers, both young and old. In addition, these reptiles only occasionally need live food, which is good news for those who don't like the thought of having to bring crickets, roaches, and other insects into their homes.

These interesting and relatively hardy lizards eat a variety of foods, are easy to maintain in very basic

set-ups, and usually settle down quickly and live for many years in captivity, growing into medium-size, submissive, approachable, and clever pets. That said, you'll need to take some simple measures right from the start if you want caring for your skink to be trouble-free.

Whether you are an advanced keeper or a beginner, this book gives you all of the information you'll need to care for and reproduce these wonderful reptiles.

CHAPTER 1

The Blue-Tongued Skink Family

Lizards, together with snakes, belong to an order of reptiles known as Squamata. On their own, lizards form the suborder Lacertilia (or Sauria), of which there are more than 4,480 species in some twenty families. They exist in greatest number and variety throughout the tropics, and they progressively lessen in number as you move farther away from the equator into the cooler temperate zones. The farther north you go, the fewer lizard species you'll see. You'll find just one, the European common or viviparous lizard (*Zootoca vivipara*), within the Arctic Circle.

Lizards are incredible reptiles that vary tremendously in both size and form. One of the world's smallest lizards, the Jaragua Sphaero (*Sphaerodactylus ariasae*), or dwarf gecko—discovered in 2001 on Beata Island off the

The dwarf gecko (*Sphaerodactylus ariasae*) is one of the world's smallest lizards.

The Komodo dragon (*Varanus komodoensis*) is one of the world's largest lizards.

southernmost point of the Dominican Republic—measures just 0.6 inches (16 mm) from its snout to the tip of its tail. At the other end of the spectrum, the giant Komodo dragon (*Varanus komodoensis*) reaches almost 10 feet (3 m) in total length and can weigh up to 330 pounds (150 kg).

Their astonishing and varied forms, vibrant and often cryptic colors and patterns, and fascinating and elaborate behavior place lizards among nature's most beautiful and extraordinary creatures. It is therefore not surprising that they are the most frequently kept exotic animals, second only to tropical fish.

Family Scincidae and Genus *Tiliqua*
One of the most diverse—and possibly the largest—of all of the lizard families is the Scincidae, the skink family, with an estimated 1,400 species in approximately fifty genera. You'll find them in the tropics and temperate zones throughout

the world, with the greatest number occurring in Africa, Southeast Asia, and Australasia. In fact, in some parts of the world—Australia especially—skinks outnumber all other lizard species.

All skinks are somewhat similar in habits and appearance, the features of any one species being fairly characteristic of the majority—namely, a fairly elongated, cylindrical body narrowing toward a comparatively short, at times even stubby, tail; a broad, pointed head; relatively small and, in most cases, highly polished scales; and short limbs. In certain species, such as the Italian three-toed skink (*Chalcides chalcides*), the limbs are so exceptionally small that they border on being absurd. Going one step further, species such as Greece's limbless skink (*Ophiomorus punctatissimus*) has, as its name suggests, no legs at all.

The most prominent, although by no means biggest, skink genus is the Australasian *Tiliqua*. These are medium

The modern blue tongue features a long cylindrical body, a stubby tail, a pointed head, and short limbs.

Classification

Kingdom: Animalia
Phylum: Chordata
Class: Reptilia
Order: Squamata
Suborder: Lacertilia (Sauria)
Infraorder: Scincomorpha
Family: Scincidae
Subfamily: Lygosominae
Genus: *Tiliqua* (Gray, 1825)

to large ground-foraging lizards—attaining lengths of up to 20 inches (50 cm) or more in some species—and include the familiar blue-tongued skinks. With the exception of the Adelaide, or Pygmy, blue-tongued skink (*Tiliqua adelaidensis*), which is for the most part a hunter of ground-dwelling crustaceans and invertebrates, all blue-tongued skinks are omnivorous, feeding on a wide range of foods from insects, gastropods, and small mammals to fruits, blossoms, and berries.

About Blue-Tongued Skinks

The *Tiliqua* genus includes several species and subspecies of blue-tongued skink, whose common name is obviously derived from its characteristic fleshy berry-blue tongue. Blue-tongued skinks are mostly large, smooth-scaled, thickset, robust lizards with comparatively short limbs; moderately sized tapering tails; large, broad, triangular heads; and dulled teeth.

Movements

The blue-tongued skink displays its distinctive tongue whenever it is suddenly threatened or alarmed. At such

To avert a threat, the blue-tongued skink turns and inflates its body to appear larger while opening its mouth wide to hiss.

times, it positions itself sideways, with its tilted body bowed, so that its head and tail are directed toward the threat. The skink inflates its body to make it look as large as possible while holding its mouth agape, tongue lolled forward, and usually hissing. This unexpected and rather startling action, often in conjunction with a strong thrash of the tail, usually succeeds in deterring rivals and predators, but the behavior usually disappears in captivity once the skink becomes tame and accustomed to movement and routine disturbances.

Although its movements are normally slow and deliberate, the blue-tongued skink can move quickly over short distances. When alarmed or threatened, for instance, it will often hold its short limbs against its body and wriggle across the ground in a snakelike manner.

Scientific Naming System

Every living thing that has ever been discovered and described is given a *scientific name*, derived from Latin or Classical Greek and consisting of two or three parts. Using this internationally recognized system helps prevent confusion caused by a species having many different common names. The assignment of scientific names to organisms is called *nomenclature* and, while these names can stand for many years, nomenclature is very fluid, and names are constantly being revised, modified, or changed.

A *species* is a wide group of similar individuals that are able to reproduce among themselves. Individuals or groups belonging to the same species are called *conspecific*. Many species are then divided into *subspecies* (organisms that have characteristic traits that differ slightly from those of their main species). Similar or related species are placed within a *genus*.

A scientific name is designated in italics and consists of the genus (in this case, *Tiliqua*) followed by the species (for example, *Tiliqua occipitalis*—the Western blue-tongued skink). A scientific name consisting of two words denotes an organism that does not have a subspecies. If a plant or animal's scientific name is three words, the third word indicates either that this is the main species of which there are subspecies or that this is a subspecies. For example: the Northern blue tongue is *Tiliqua scincoides intermedia*, a subspecies of the Eastern blue tongue *Tiliqua scincoides scincoides*. A species with the same name repeated twice is the main species, or the pure breed. A subspecies of the Eastern blue tongue is the Kei Island blue tongue, and its scientific name is *Tiliqua scincoides keyensis*.

So, in summary:

First word = genus name (*Tiliqua*)
Second word = species name (*gigas*)
Third word (if the same) = main species (*gigas*)
Third word (if different) = subspecies name (*keyensis*)

Habits and Life Expectancy

As with the rest of the genus, the blue-tongued skink is diurnal, spending the daylight hours foraging for food and engaging in its other routine activities, such as basking, defending its territory, courting, and breeding. Although it will occasionally crawl into the lower, thicker branches of shrubs in its search for food and haul itself onto rocky ledges from time to time to bask, its short limbs are not adapted for climbing.

The fact that the blue tongue has a nonspecialized diet means that it can occupy a surprisingly wide variety of habitats. It can live in areas from grassland to semiarid brush scrub, from open forest to rock-strewn steppe. It is also

Like many other lizards, blue tongues seek out sunny spots atop rocks or other objects to bask for a period of time.

equally at home on the margins of both subhumid tropical forest and semidesert.

During midday, when the sun is at its hottest, the blue tongue seeks out shade and shelter in deserted animal burrows, in rocky crevices, among the roots of trees, in hollow logs, or beneath stones, dead vegetation, or other natural or man-made debris. The skink often uses these same retreats as sleeping quarters at night, when its somewhat flattened body enables it to hide itself easily in such places.

The normal life expectancy for this species in captivity is between fifteen and twenty years, although there are unconfirmed reports of individuals living beyond thirty-two years. Scientists have yet to determine a blue tongue's longevity in the wild.

CHAPTER 2

Common Blue-Tongued Skinks

Throughout the pages of this book, you'll see references to individual species. While a particular breed may have a reputation for being placid, easy to handle, ideal for the beginner, or good with children, there is always an exception to the rule. A great deal of your skink's behavior will depend on how you keep it and how often and how carefully you handle it. That said, getting to know the different species a bit better before you buy a skink will help ensure that you'll be happy with your choice.

Wild blue-tongued skinks are confined entirely to Australasia, with six types occurring on mainland Australia itself: the Western (*Tiliqua occipitalis*), the Centralian (*T. multifasciata*), the Eastern (*T. scincoides scincoides*), the Northern (*T. s. intermedia*), the Blotched (*T. nigrolutea* [the only species to occur in Tasmania]), and the Pygmy (*T. adelaidensis*). The Indonesian blue-tongued skink, *T. gigas gigas*, occurs in Papua New Guinea and on a few Indonesian islands with two subspecies: the Kei Island (*T. g. keyensis*) and the Merauke (*T. g. evanescens)*.

Indonesian Blue-Tongued Skink, *Tiliqua gigas gigas*

This species is sometimes known as the New Guinea blue tongue, and it is one of the most familiar and commonly kept blue-tongued skinks. It is also known in some parts as the great Moluccan skink, although this name is not often used today. This species can be found in Papua New Guinea, Jobi, the Admiralty Islands, New Britain, and the Bismarck Archipelago.

Under optimal conditions, this skink can grow

The Indonesian blue tongue (*Tiliqua gigas gigas*).

extremely rapidly. Newborn Indonesian blue tongues measure roughly 6 inches (15 cm) in length from head to tail and can double in length every four weeks or so during their first few months of life. In just eighteen to twenty months, they can reach their full adult size of 19.75 inches (50 cm); those inhabiting the Sarong region can grow even longer.

In most New Guinea blue-tongued skinks, the ground color ranges from a golden yellow to a light brown or sometimes a light, almost silvery gray or gray-brown. Most are dappled with fifteen to twenty slender, dark, irregularly shaped bands across the back and tail. These bands may become indistinct or be absent on the tail, which is frequently completely black with occasionally a little speckling of white or brown. Specimens inhabiting the islands of Ceram and Ambon are virtually solid black all over, with little or no brown.

The *venter*, or underside, can range from cream to orange and may be peppered with black. The short limbs are usually entirely glossy black and may be spotted with white. The large scales on the broad triangular head are very often edged in black, and a single black stripe usually runs down the center of the back of the neck. Occasionally, a dark stripe extends from the neck to the tail. The tongue is, obviously, a vivid berry-blue color and may protrude and roll forward from the deep pink interior of the mouth during a show of aggression.

Two subspecies are recognized: the Kei Island blue-tongued skink (*T. g. keyensis*), and the Merauke blue-tongued skink (*T. g. evanescens*).

Kei Island Blue-Tongued Skink, *Tiliqua gigas keyensis*

The Kei Island blue-tongued skink, as its name suggests, occurs on the Indonesian Kei Islands. Keis start developing their adult colors at around two to three months of age. The ground color, although quite variable, is typically greenish, with spots and bands of black or brown mixed with reds, browns, and tans; some specimens also display yellows and oranges. The tip of this blue tongue's nose (on a rather stout head) is almost always creamy to white.

The Kei differs from the New Guinea subspecies in several ways: Individual Kei specimens are more impressively built and are therefore more energetic and more active. Kei blue tongues have faded and spotted bands (compared to the

The Kei Island blue-tongued skink (*Tiliqua gigas keyensis*).

New Guinea's well-defined banding) and very pale orange, or even white, bellies (compared to the New Guinea's darker, often red, stomach). In addition, Keis always have the same markings on their flanks no matter what color they are, whereas the New Guinea blue tongues lack this pattern. Lastly, the Kei's head is exceptional and, rather than tapering to a tip, has a nose that comes to an abrupt point.

Merauke Blue-Tongued Skink, *Tiliqua gigas evanescens*

The Merauke blue-tongued skink, known also as the Faded blue tongue, occurs in southern Papua New Guinea and is the longest of the blue tongues. The Merauke often attains

The Merauke blue tongue (*Tiliqua gigas evanescens*).

17

lengths of more than 25 inches (63.5 cm), with some adult specimens reaching 30 inches (76 cm).

Juvenile Merauke individuals can sometimes be very tricky to differentiate from New Guinea blue tongues. Generally speaking, though, the Merauke has several features that help in its identification: It has a huge tail that is usually much longer than that of the typical New Guinea. Although many specimens display a faded grey tinge (hence its alternative name), both the tail and the body are generally fresher, and the striped pattern more distinct. The Merauke's throat lacks any speckling, and its forelegs usually lack the solid black found in the New Guinea.

Although it might not be as eye-catching as some other blue-tongued species, the Merauke can, even if infrequently, show impressive coloration. Generally, though, the species makes up for lack of visual impact by having a pleasantly placid disposition.

Centralian Blue-Tongued Skink, *Tiliqua multifasciata*

The Centralian, or Central, blue-tongued skink occurs in both desert and tropical habitats, including coastal sand dunes, open shrublands, woodlands, and hummock grasslands in West Australia, Queensland, South Australia, and the Northern Territory. It can attain an average total length of 15.5 to 17.5 inches (40 to 45 cm) and has the characteristic blue-tongue build: a robust body; a large,

The Centralian blue tongue (*Tiliqua multifasciata*).

Irian Jaya

Irian Jaya is the former name of the province of West Papua in Indonesia that occupies the western half of New Guinea and a dozen offshore islands. At the time of writing, one more species of blue tongue, which has been recognized for over a decade but has yet to be scientifically described, exists there. This skink is currently known as the Irian Jaya or West Papuan blue-tongued skink. With the region's thousands of tropical and often isolated constituent islands, additional forms of the blue-tongued skink may be discovered before long.

The Irian Jaya (*Tiliqua Sp.*).

triangular head; and a relatively short tail. The Centralian's color is predominately brownish gray with eleven to thirteen narrow orange bands across the length of the body and wider brown bands across the tail.

Active by day, the Centralian hunts for invertebrates and small mammals and forages for plants and berries. At night, it seeks refuge in unused animal burrows or beneath leaves, rock piles, logs, and so on. Females give birth to between two and six young, which is a relatively low rate among blue tongues. The Centralian is listed as "Vulnerable" under the New South Wales

The Eastern blue-tongued skink (*Tiliqua scincoides scincoides*).

Threatened Species Conservation Act 1995, which categorizes threatened species into three groups—Critically Endangered, Endangered, and Vulnerable—by risk of extinction.

Eastern Blue-Tongued Skink, *Tiliqua scincoides scincoides*

Sometimes known as the common blue-tongued lizard, the Eastern blue-tongued skink inhabits a wide range of environments, including bushland, montane forest, semi-desert, and cultivated areas, and it even appears occasionally in suburban gardens in Victoria, southeastern South Australia, New South Wales, and southern Queensland. This stout and slow-moving lizard, which is extremely hardy and can live for up to thirty years in captivity, grows to an average length of 19 inches (48 cm), although larger specimens have been recorded. The Eastern's diet includes invertebrates, small mammals, and plant material.

This blue tongue is extremely variable in color but usually has a grayish to orange-brown ground color with darker bars extending over the back onto the flanks and sometimes continuing onto the pale underside. The scales between these bands are generally marked with dark lateral edges, forming a sequence of thin, dark brown, arrowlike lines that extend the length of the body. A dark brown or black temporal strip runs from the back of the eye to the top of the ear opening on each side. The skink's forelimbs are basically patternless and are always much lighter in color than the hind limbs. Finally, the Eastern has a fat tail and a comparatively narrow head.

The Northern blue tongue (*Tiliqua scincoides intermedia*).

Northerns are the largest of the blue tongues. Here, a Northern baby is compared to a Tanimbar baby.

Two subspecies are currently recognized: the Northern blue-tongued skink (*T. s. intermedia*) and the Tanimbar Island blue-tongued skink (*T. s. chimaerea*).

Northern Blue-Tongued Skink, *Tiliqua scincoides intermedia*

Native to Australia, the Northern blue-tongued skink is confined almost entirely to the savannah and tropical woodlands of the Northern Territory and lives an average of twenty years. The Northern skink is very likely the largest and heaviest member of the *Tiliqua* genus, attaining an average length of 24 inches (61 cm). Despite their large size, Northerns are commonly kept as pets because of their docile temperaments. Females typically give birth to between four and twenty live young.

Comparable in shape to the other members of the genus *Tiliqua*, the Northern blue tongue has very characteristic patterning: a vivid to soft peachy-orange or even a yellowish color with darker stripes along its back and flanks. The lizard's underparts are usually a paler, creamier color. Adults and neonates (babies) usually have only negligible differences in their markings and coloration.

Tanimbar Island Blue-Tongued Skink, *Tiliqua scincoides chimaerea*

Occasionally known as the Sunda blue-tongued skink, this species is limited solely to the Tanimbar (also known as Timor Laut) and Baber Island groups at the lower end of the Makulu Island chain (formerly the Moluccas) in Indonesia. A small species, the adults range in size from 15 to 17 inches (38 to 43 cm). Adult female Tanimbars typically produce litters of up to ten live young, all miniature replicas of their parents.

The extremely smooth scales of the Tanimbar Island blue-tongued skink are shiny and almost glasslike. The body color is typically a golden brown banded with silvery

The Tanimbar Island blue-tongued skink (*Tiliqua scincoides chimaerea*).

gray. However, this coloration can range from vivid orange to lemon yellow to pure white. With age, many specimens become an overall silvery color. This skink's belly is a golden yellow that extends onto its throat and chin. The forelimbs are, on the whole, devoid of any pattern and lighter in color than the hind limbs. The head lacks any speckling, and there is no temporal streak between the eye and ear.

The Tanimbar's scientific subspecies name *chimaerea* refers to the Chimaera, a fire-breathing she-monster from Greek mythology that was a combination of a lion, a goat, and a snake. The Tanimbar was given this scientific name because of its extreme aggressiveness, which differs greatly from the serene temperament customarily associated with other blue-tongued skinks. If handled frequently when young, captive Tanimbar specimens can become tame to a certain degree; however, this species is not recommended as a pet for children.

Blotched Blue-Tongued Skink, *Tiliqua nigrolutea*

The Blotched blue-tongued skink, also known as the Black and Yellow blue tongue and Southern blue tongue, is a

The Blotched blue tongue (*Tiliqua nigrolutea*).

robust and relatively large member of the *Tiliqua* genus and an inhabitant of New South Wales, South Australia, Victoria, and Tasmania. It resides in both wet and dry environments from coastal heaths to mountain forests. Blotched blue tongues also visit suburban gardens, where the owners welcome them for controlling pests such as snails and slugs.

This species can grow up to 23.5 inches (60 cm) in length. It is omnivorous, feeding on a variety of insects, spiders, arthropods, and plants. An inquisitive lizard, the Blotched blue tongue tames easily and is long-lived. Females produce three to ten live young and frequently interbreed with members of the *T. scincoides* species.

As far as coloring goes, this is an unusual species among blue tongues because it is dark brown to black with yellowing and many irregular blotches down its back and tail. Two distinct forms of this species—a lowland form and a highland, or alpine, form—seem to exist. The alpine variety is usually larger and inclined to have brighter, more colorful pink or orange blotches on its back whereas the lowland type is darker with darker markings. The tail of this species is particularly fat and comes to a sudden point instead of tapering.

Western Blue-Tongued Skink
Tiliqua occipitalis

The Western blue-tongued skink is found chiefly in Western Australia. In the Northern Territory, it is limited to the far south, and in South Australia, it is separated into western and eastern populations. This species is usually found in dry areas, such as shrublands, grasslands, scrubby woodlands, and dunes. It is omnivorous and active by day, hunting for insects, spiders, and snails, the shells of which it crushes in its strong jaws. The Western blue tongue will also browse for plants (especially fruit-bearing) and carrion. It spends nights in deserted rabbit warrens or beneath rocks, logs, or leaves. The average Western grows to be around 19.5 inches (50 cm) in length. Females give birth to five to ten brown-and-yellow-banded live young, which are almost

The Western blue-tongued skink (*Tiliqua occipitalis*).

immediately independent.

Like most members of its family, the Western blue-tongued skink is typically heavy bodied and short limbed with a broad, triangular head and short tail. A distinctive black marking adorns the rear of each eye. Its ground color is generally dark tan or reddish brown with paler banding across the body and tail; the underside of the body is usually pale.

Like the Central blue tongue, the Western is listed as "Vulnerable" according to the NSW Threatened Species Conservation Act 1995. The main threats to the species are clearance of its habitat for agriculture and the subsequent destruction of the rabbit warrens upon which the skinks depend for refuge, as well as predation by the domestic cat and introduced species such as the European red fox. Because it is one of the rarer species of blue tongue, the Western is seldom kept as a pet.

Pygmy Blue-Tongued Skink, *Tiliqua scincoides adelaidensis*

Also known as the Dwarf blue-tongued skink, the Pygmy, as its name suggests, is the smallest of the *Tiliqua* genus, seldom attaining a length of more than 4 inches (10 cm). It is found only in the grasslands of Adelaide in

A Blue-Tongued Relative

One other equally fascinating *Tiliqua* species occurs in Australia: the Stump-tailed skink, *T. rugosa*. Known also by the names of sleepy lizard, bobtail, and shingleback skink, this slow-moving lizard is closely related to the blue-tongued skinks, with similar habits and a stunning triangular cobalt-blue tongue.

The Stump-tailed skink reaches roughly 12 inches (30 cm) in length; has a short, flattened tail that strongly resembles its head in both shape and size; and has huge, rough, more ossified, and keeled scales (it's often likened to a pine cone). Recent research suggests that this species is monogamous, and a pair may stay together for twenty years or longer. Gestation lasts for about five months, and adult females give birth to just one to three very big young.

Several varieties of the Stump-tailed skink can be found in Queensland, New South Wales, South Australia, Victoria, and West Australia. They differ in color from an overall jet black to a dark brown with speckled white, yellow, or orange spots (on their flanks in particular).

The Stump-tailed skink (*Tiliqua rugosa*).

Australia and lives belowground, usually in the burrows of wolf and trapdoor spiders, where it can be easily overlooked. In fact, in the early 1930s, the Pygmy blue tongue had been so rarely seen that it was thought to have become extinct, only to be rediscovered some sixty years later in 1992.

The Pygmy is pale grayish or gray-brown in color and speckled with darker spots and blotches, with no real stripes or patterns. It has a very slim, short tail; short limbs; and a disproportionately large head compared to its body. Adult males have wider heads but are shorter than females. Females give birth to between one and five young. Unlike the other members of the genus, the Pygmy has a pink tongue.

The Pygmy is extremely rare—scientists believe that only about five thousand exist in the wild today—although efforts are currently underway to increase its numbers. It is illegal to privately own a Pygmy blue-tongued skink and, in fact, only two organizations in Australia are known to have them: the Adelaide Zoo has a small breeding group, and the South Australian Museum has an adult male.

CHAPTER 3

Before You Buy

S o you have your heart set on keeping a blue-tongued skink. Before you go out and get one, you need to consider a few things. Simply put, are you going to have the time, commitment, space, and funds to care for this animal for at least a decade, possibly two or more?

Unlike many other pets, lizards do not need a lot of physical interaction with humans—in fact, most of them do not appreciate attention, preferring to be left alone. Even so, when kept in an artificial and captive environment, they need to be watched closely and checked frequently to ensure that they are not showing signs of injury or illness. And, of course, they also need food and clean cages.

A captive reptile's or amphibian's cage can be called many names. In order to avoid confusion, this book will refer to an indoor cage as a *vivarium* and an outdoor one as an *enclosure*.

Unlike with cats and dogs, which you can find easily and whose care is pretty well known, you'll have to do a bit more research before buying your lizard.

Skink-Owning Advantages

While you have to consider all of the possible problems associated with keeping a blue-tongued skink, you shouldn't forget the advantages of owning this species. The blue-tongued skink doesn't require a lot of space, it won't scratch off your wallpaper or chew on your furniture, it doesn't have to be taken out for walks, it doesn't need to be entertained, it doesn't require a lot of food, and it's unlikely to make any noise that will annoy the neighbors.

Blue-tongued skinks can live for between ten and twenty years, which is longer than many dogs live. So, as with a puppy, you should be prepared to make a long-term commitment when you consider taking on one of these lizards. The worst thing you can do is think, "I'll keep one for a year or two and see how things go. If I don't like it, I'll get rid of it." "Trying out" a skink would be a waste of your time and money, and more importantly, it would be very stressful to the skink. Furthermore, under no circumstances should you keep any reptile solely to make an impression on friends or because it is "different."

During your skink's life with you, your personal circumstances may change. In fact, over a twenty-year period, it would be surprising if they didn't. For example, you may expand your family, or you might move to another, perhaps smaller, house or apartment. Give the matter of acquiring a skink some careful thought and remember that, as with cats and dogs, too many unwanted and abandoned reptiles—skinks included—languish in animal rescues across the country.

Cost Considerations

Compared to the expense of buying and keeping a dog, a blue-tongued skink is almost a bargain. Even so, you need to consider not only the initial costs but also the price of caring for your skink throughout its long life. The following sections will help you figure out whether you can handle the expense, as well as how to keep it to a minimum.

Initial Outlay

Prices vary for blue-tongued skinks, but you can expect to pay anywhere from fifty dollars up to a few hundred dollars for one. A lot depends on whether it is wild-caught or captive-bred, the latter being more desirable and therefore fetching a higher price.

The skink's vivarium and its associated heating and lighting equipment may exceed the cost of the skink itself many times over; however, we are talking about only the *initial* outlay here. After you've purchased the lizard and all of the items necessary for its well-being—the vivarium, one or more heat lamps, an ultraviolet light tube or bulb, electrical accessories, a water bowl, vivarium decorations, an initial supply of food, and so on—the actual long-term cost of maintaining and caring for this species is fairly reasonable.

Maintenance Costs

Once you've purchased the vivarium and everything needed to set it up, the costs of maintaining it are low. You won't see a significant increase in your electric bill from your vivarium's heating and lighting, and you'll need to buy only disinfectants and fresh substrate when you clean the vivarium.

As for food, your skink just needs a little of the fruit, vegetables, meat, or fish that you serve yourself for your own meals. And if you live in a somewhat rural area, you can cut your food costs significantly by collecting wild plants and fruit—such as dandelions, clovers, blackberries, and blueberries—from areas that have not been sprayed by any harmful chemicals, such as insecticides or herbicides. A small quantity of insects, and perhaps a few frozen baby

Shopping List

The following list gives you an idea of the basic items that you'll need from the outset. More detailed explanations of each piece of equipment, as well as discussions on optional accessories, can be found in chapter 5.

☐ The skink

☐ A suitably sized vivarium

☐ A method of heating the vivarium (cables, pads, infrared emitter) to the temperature of your skink's natural environment

☐ Lighting (and its associated accessories) to illuminate the vivarium and benefit the lizard's health

☐ Thermostats, timers, dimmer switches, and thermometers for regulating and maintaining temperatures and controlling lighting

☐ A water bowl

☐ Items the lizard can retreat to, in, or under (hide box, hollow logs, pieces of bark)

☐ Substrate, such as sand, gravel, or bark chippings

☐ Artificial plants, branches, and other decorations (if desired)

☐ Vitamin and mineral supplements

☐ Appropriate fresh or frozen fruits and vegetables

All your blue tongue really needs to be happy in its vivarium is some substrate, a bit of "furniture," water, and some skink-friendly food.

rodents, from your local pet-supply shop once a week will not cost much.

The only other expense that you may face from time to time is an unexpected veterinary bill should your skink become ill or injured. It's always a good idea to budget for such an eventuality. You can read about how to find a veterinarian and what to expect in chapter 9.

Keeping Expenses Down

Although you'll have to get up early in the morning, it might be worth the effort to check out local garage sales or flea markets in search of an aquarium tank that you can convert into a vivarium. Even a damaged tank that's unsuitable for fish can be perfect for a land-dwelling reptile. With a little modification and a thorough scrub-down with an animal-friendly disinfectant, your skink can have a new (heavily discounted) home. The Internet is another great source for used and discounted housing items. Try searching auction websites, online classified ads, and sites that allow you to barter for goods rather than buy them.

Seeking out nontraditional sources can also help you find substrate material and other items for inside your skink's vivarium. In addition to your local pet supply store, take a look in craft, hobby, and charity stores, as well as in home and garden centers, all of which may offer items that you can use right out of the package or with some creative modifications.

You can also save money on the purchase of the skink itself. Try to find a young skink, which typically will be much cheaper than a mature adult. In addition, buy your skink locally so that you can see what's being offered before you buy, and you won't have to spend money on shipping costs. If you do make a long-distance purchase, find out whether it's cheaper to collect your new pet yourself or arrange for a courier to collect it for you.

Cutting food costs is as simple as putting your green thumb to use. In addition to collecting edible berries and wild plants (as mentioned earlier), try your hand at growing your own fruits and vegetables. If you don't have the space for a garden, you can grow many plants in small window boxes or even indoors. While you're at it, raise your own colony of insects, such as crickets or mealworms, and keep a breeding pair of mice, which will provide you with babies every month or so.

You don't have to spend a ton of money to create a great living environment for your skink. Consider shopping online, at yard sales, and at discount pet stores.

Doing the Research

Whether you are a beginning or an advanced reptile keeper, learn as much as you can about the species you intend to keep *before* you obtain it. Too many people rush into getting a reptile without any forethought. Consequently, they just as quickly realize that they cannot provide the necessary time, conditions, or facilities to properly care for their new pet. Just a little research and preparation beforehand will go a long way toward avoiding difficulties and heartache later and, perhaps more importantly, preventing stress and suffering to the animal concerned. So, before you do anything else, at least read this manual from cover to cover.

In addition to reading up on the subject, you should do some field research. Visit the reptile house at your local zoo to see what sort of setup they provide for their reptiles and, if they have them, for blue-tongued skinks in particular. Zookeepers are often more than willing to give advice or help to anyone with a genuine interest in the animals they care for.

If you can't find someone with firsthand blue-tongue experience to speak to in person, pick up the phone, send an e-mail, or even write a letter (including a self-addressed stamped envelope should encourage a reply). Contact the head reptile keepers at zoos or independent reptile keepers and breeders.

Take Your Time

Never rush into acquiring a blue-tongued skink—remember, it may live for more than twenty years. That's a long time, so you need to minimize the chances of regretting your choice. Once you have decided on the purchase, progress carefully, taking note of the advice given in this book. By thoughtfully considering all of the factors that should go into your decision, you also accrue valuable information about the particular blue-tongued skink you wish to keep and its requirements.

Visiting the reptile exhibit at your local zoo is a great way to gather information on blue tongues and their relatives.

The Internet can help you find experienced skink keepers; search for reptile-related clubs and societies in your area. Even if your initial contacts don't keep blue-tongued skinks personally, they might be able to put you in touch with others who do. Plus, members of reputable organizations are usually very good sources of healthy, good-quality captive-bred stock.

The Last Stop

Once you have read all you can and have asked all of the relevant questions, ask yourself the following:

- Can I commit to an animal that may live for twenty years?
- Can I provide a vivarium or enclosure from which a skink cannot escape and in which it will live a long, healthy, and stress-free life?
- Taking into account all of the expenses of buying and raising a skink, can I afford one?
- Will my family and friends accept the presence of a reptile in my home?
- Can I devote sufficient time to feeding, cleaning, and other necessary routine tasks?
- Will I be able to find someone who will give my skink the necessary care when I am on vacation?

If you answered no to any of these questions, you should seriously re-examine whether a blue-tongued skink is right for you—and whether you are right for it. If, however, you can answer yes to all of the above, and your motives are good, then feel free to proceed with your purchase.

CHAPTER 4

Obtaining Your Skink

Y ou can often prevent the health and behavioral problems encountered in animals, including blue-tongued skinks, by seeking advice before you acquire your new pet. Think carefully about the sex, age, housing and feeding needs, health care, and general origins of the skinks that you're considering. Being well versed in the different species and knowing how to go about obtaining a skink will help you not only decide on the best pet for your home but also get ready for the new arrival beforehand.

Reptile Keeping and the Law

Most countries have some form of federal, state, and/or local legislation governing not only the importation and exportation of animals—reptiles included—but also the keeping and transportation of them. These rules and regulations change regularly and differ from country to country, from state to state. The commercial importation and sale of certain species may be restricted, or even banned, in some regions. Check your local laws before obtaining a skink to ensure that you are legally able to own one.

Finding a Supplier

You should be able to find pet stores in your area by looking in the phone book or doing an Internet search. Specialist magazines will list reptile breeders who have blue-tongued skinks for sale. And don't overlook reptile-rescue groups, animal shelters, and other animal-welfare organizations, both local and national. Rescues often have blue-tongued skinks that need good homes.

The Internet gives you the ability to find and buy things that are not available to you locally. But, if you do decide

Buying a juvenile skink allows you the opportunity to watch it grow.

to make your purchase online, use caution. Many reptile breeders keep impressive websites detailing lengthy lists of exotic species. The majority of them have many years of experience in keeping and breeding a variety of reptiles; they are reliable and trustworthy, with long-established reputations that they are eager to protect. Unfortunately, there are also some sellers out there who are not very honest and do not appear to be concerned with the well-being of their animals—their only concern is making a fast buck. The old saying "a photograph never lies" could not be further from the truth these days. Computer software makes it easy to alter photos, including distorting the subject, changing colors, and many other tricks. Be careful not to be fooled by sellers who advertise "exciting" and "rare" color varieties or who purport to breed unusually marked individuals. If you see a listing that looks interesting, request more photographs and information—ask about the skink's origins, how old it is, what it is eating, and so on. If you receive short or implausible replies, or no reply at all, think twice before buying from this person. A reputable breeder or seller should be more than pleased to give you as much information as possible, including photographs.

Juvenile or Adult?

Generally speaking, most buyers prefer juvenile skinks less than 8 inches (20 cm) long to adults because—if for no other reason—they can watch their pets grow and develop. Almost all available juvenile blue-tongued skinks will have been captive bred, but it's likely that the majority of adults offered for sale were either caught in the wild or are past their prime. The latter is particularly true of long-term captives that have been used in intensive breeding programs. This type of skink can sometimes have its advantages; however, it should be healthy, feeding well, and accustomed to being handled.

If you choose to buy an adult, ask the seller why he or she is selling it. Ask to see its health and behavior records, if the owner has them. You might discover that your prospective skink has been giving its owner problems—problems that you don't want to deal with. Maybe it's an imported wild-caught creature that hasn't adapted to captivity. Or you might find out that the skink is nearing the end of its life. Only proceed with the purchase if you're happy with the information you've received and the skink is alert, is active, and appears to be in good health.

Choosing a Healthy Reptile

Seeing the skink you intend to buy in person is always better than obtaining one "blind," such as from an online source or by mail order. As mentioned, while many highly regarded commercial dealers and private breeders offer good-quality, healthy stock sight-unseen, not all breeders and sellers are scrupulous businesspeople. In any case, having your

Male or Female?

In the company of other skinks, both sexes can be aggressive toward each other. Individually, however, no obvious differences in disposition exist between the sexes. Unless you intend to eventually breed your pet, personal preference is all that matters when deciding whether to get a male or female blue tongue.

If you can, try to handle potential blue tongues in person before you buy one.

skink shipped to you may sometimes be your only option, particularly if the nearest supplier is many miles away. Get recommendations from trusted friends and others in the hobby, and make sure that the seller has a good reputation.

If you're lucky enough to have a breeder within driving distance, you can make a personal visit and glean all kinds of information. You may be able to examine and handle several individuals, and you can talk to the breeder about the reptiles' temperaments, husbandry requirements, and food preferences. Even if it's a long journey, the time and expense of visiting a dealer or breeder is far better than the disappointment of receiving a reptile that looks nothing like it did in the advertisement or, worse, is dehydrated, sickly, or dead.

Conduct a Physical

When you visit the seller, ask if you can handle the skink. Give the lizard a thorough once-over with your hands and eyes. If, at this early stage, you are a little apprehensive about holding a skink, ask the seller if he or she will hold it so that you can at least take a close look at it. A healthy skink will have a full, firm-looking body, and its skin will have a nice sheen and be free of scars, injuries, and unsloughed skin fragments. If you can see the lizard's spine or ribs protruding through its skin, something is wrong.

Carefully go over the skink's body, looking for any signs of illness, injury, or personality issues.

Remember, a healthy skink is an active skink, and it should be taking as much of an interest in you as you are in it. It should be flicking its tongue in and out and "tasting" your hands as you allow it to move freely within your grasp. While you're handling the skink, be aware of any lumps, bumps, or nodules beneath its skin; these could be cysts or tumors. Any slight dents or depressions, particularly around the ribs or spine, could be indicative of broken bones.

Looking at the lizard's head, its nostrils should be dry and not blocked with bubbly mucus, which could indicate an upper respiratory infection. Its eyes should be bright and clear, with no encrustation on the lids. A skink whose eyes are partially or completely closed most of the time is *not* a healthy skink. Try to encourage the skink to open its mouth by tapping it very gently on its snout or carefully pulling the skin underneath its lower jaw (with some individuals, such assistance may not be necessary!). Bubbly mucus inside the mouth indicates a possible respiratory infection. In very severe cases, you may see mucus at the corners of the closed mouth and coming from the nostrils. Reject any skink with these symptoms.

While the lizard's mouth is open, ensure that the gums and the linings of its mouth look pink and healthy and are free from ulcerations. Any redness or injuries could be indications of stomatitis, otherwise known as *mouth rot* or *canker*. Stomatitis is a bacterial infection of the oral cavity that typically results from a mouth injury, stress, inferior husbandry, or a combination of these and other circumstances. In acute cases, the teeth and gums become encrusted with cheeselike pus.

After examining the mouth, ask to see your prospective pet eat. Provided that the skink isn't full from a recent meal, any reluctance to feed could suggest a problem. If it attempts to grasp its food but fails each time, and its lower jaw looks weak or rubbery, it is almost certainly suffering from a vitamin/mineral deficiency. Unless you have experience in treating sick reptiles, it is best to look for a healthier specimen.

Body Check

The blue-tongued skink you bring home with you should have passed your physical examination with flying colors. To sum up, make sure you've checked the following areas:

☐ Eyes, ears, and nose—should be clear and clean with no signs of discharge

☐ Skin—should be healthy and free from injury, parasites, and unsloughed fragments

☐ Anal region—should be clean with no mucus or encrustation

☐ Limbs—should be strong, straight, and able to support the body

☐ Feet—should have five toes each

☐ Tail—should be unbroken and tapered to a point

Make sure that the skink's underside is free of blisters and discolored, elevated, or broken ventral scales, all of which are symptomatic of disease. The anal plate covering the vent (the opening to the cloaca [anus]) should rest flat against the body and be clean and free of any caked matter. Also inspect your potential skink for strong, able limbs; feet with all five toes; and an unbroken, tapered tail.

Finally, scrutinize the vivarium or enclosure in which the skink is being kept. Smeared blood and watery feces are indications of intestinal problems. Look for any signs of parasites (see the next section). If the living area is covered in waste and grime, think twice about buying one of the skinks that live in it. A clean vivarium/enclosure—and a

Check your prospective pet for signs of parasites such as ticks (seen here) and mites.

clean establishment overall—tells you a great deal about the seller and the animals being offered.

Check for Parasites

Detecting the presence of internal parasites from an external examination is nearly impossible, but if you suspect them for some reason, you should take the skink to a veterinarian for screening and potential treatment. External parasites, such as ticks and mites, are comparatively easy to detect and treat.

Ticks are relatively common among all creatures, including humans. They attach themselves via their mouthparts to the thin interstitial skin between lizards' scales. Unfed, this parasite is flat and often appears in size, shape, and color very much like one of the lizard's scales. Over a period of a few hours, the tick's body bloats as it feeds on the lizard's blood. Finally, engorged, it falls off and wanders away to lay its eggs.

Skinks born and reared in captivity will normally not have ticks unless they have come into contact with imported

Ticks

Ticks are found throughout the temperate and tropical world. They are moderately large, rounded, eight-legged, blood-sucking arachnids—relatives of spiders—and attach themselves to the skin of many animals, including reptiles. A tick does not bite its host; rather, it harpoons its sharp proboscis into the host's body.

Most ticks live from as little as a week to as long as six months or more, depending on the climatic conditions. They do not leap or fly but move in a slow crawl. A tick typically sits at the end of a blade of grass, a branch, or some other object and waits for an animal to brush past, at which point it quickly clings to the animal. A tick can, however, travel up to 16 feet (5 meters) to actively search for a host.

lizards or others already infested. If you are planning to house your skink in an outdoor enclosure, even temporarily, you will have to check it regularly to make sure it has not picked up one or more of these arachnids.

Ticks can transmit disease and can also greatly weaken an animal if not promptly removed. If you see them on the skinks you are visiting or notice them crawling from the vivarium, ask the breeder or seller if he or she will remove them for you; otherwise, you will have to do it yourself when you get home (see page 108 for more information). Generally speaking, once any ticks have been removed, the host animal will be fine.

Mites, the other common ectoparasite of many snakes and lizards, are chiefly found in the wild but also occur frequently in captivity. Like ticks, they are arachnids, but unlike ticks, they are tiny—not much bigger than one of the periods on this page. You may find mites on any part of a reptile's body, but they have a tendency to cluster on the head, especially around the nostrils and eyes.

Also like ticks, mites feed on the blood of their hosts. If not eradicated, they quickly multiply, and heavy infestations can seriously weaken a reptile, eventually resulting in its death. Mites are reddish brown to black in color and can usually be observed either moving on the lizard's body or entrenched around the eyelids. Another surefire sign of mites on the reptile you were handling? Finding several crawling on your hands afterward.

If you're not sure if a skink has mites, check for very tiny white or grayish flecks on the lizard's skin. These are the mite's waste products, which suggest that the lizard has been, or still is, infested. Unless you can isolate and treat the reptile immediately, think twice about getting a mite-infested lizard—especially if you have other mite-free reptiles in your collection.

Getting Your Pet Home

You've selected an alert, active, and healthy-looking skink; you've asked all of the relevant questions; and you've parted

Though it's hard to resist getting to know your new blue tongue right away, give it time to acclimate to its new surroundings.

with your money. Now all you have to do is get your new pet home.

How you transport your new skink to your home is surprisingly important. Stressed skinks are not healthy skinks, and any animal—humans included—can become stressed by a move, especially if it is not used to traveling. Making the journey as comfortable and as easy as possible is vital.

Place your skink in a tough cloth bag—one made of cotton or muslin is ideal—with some crumpled newspaper or chunks of soft foam rubber to prevent it from being knocked around. Knot the neck of the bag or secure it with a piece of string or tape and place it in a sturdy box. The box should have small holes in it for ventilation and more crumpled paper or pieces of foam rubber for packing, and it should be secured shut. All reptiles, be they snakes, lizards, or even chelonians, are traditionally transported this way. They relax and are comfortable in the bags, which contain sufficient air for the animals to survive for several days. The bags prevent the reptiles from injuring themselves on the sharp corners and hard sides of the boxes in which they are placed, and the boxes prevent the bags—and the creatures they contain—from being accidentally crushed.

Depending on the part of the world in which you live and the prevailing temperature at the time, providing warmth may be an important consideration while your skink is in transit. If you live in a colder climate, you may need to do away with the box and keep the lizard in its bag next to your body, in your pocket, or beneath your clothing. Instant hot packs, intended for sports injuries and other such applications, are ideal for keeping your skink warm on the journey. Their compact size makes these single-use packs ideal to take anywhere. Alternatively, you can place a rubber water bottle filled with warm water in the bottom of the skink's travelling box and rest the bag on top of it.

Always keep in mind that not everyone shares your enthusiasm for lizards. Do not, whatever you do, remove your new skink from its bag or carrying box while in public. If you are taking public transportation, your fellow passengers will not enjoy having their ride interrupted by the unexpected emergence of your blue-tongued skink—regardless of how fascinating and beautiful *you* think it is. Nor should you walk down the street with the skink in your hands. Even if it doesn't cause alarm, it could

Wild-Caught Skinks

Some snake species taken from the wild require several weeks, even months, to settle down in captivity. Thankfully, this is rarely the case with lizards, which seem to adapt much more quickly. However, if your skink was wild-caught, it will certainly need several weeks to settle into captivity.

Any newly acquired wild-caught blue-tongued skink should be quarantined for a six-to-eight-week period. A veterinarian who is experienced with reptiles should screen and treat it for internal parasites and any other ailments during this time. Remember, external parasites such as mites and ticks, despite their relatively small size, can travel a significant distance and will quickly infest otherwise healthy specimens. If you own other reptiles, isolate your new addition from them, preferably in another room to ensure that all of your pets are protected.

Internal parasites, such as flukes, roundworms, and tapeworms, can all occur in wild-caught reptiles and occasionally in captive-bred ones too. Various protozoans, such as *Entamoeba*, for example, can also be present and can cause slimy, watery, and sometimes bloody feces; a refusal to feed; and an urge to drink often. An unhealthy reptile that gets proper treatment will almost always settle down in captivity more quickly than one that does not receive treatment.

still escape your grasp and injure itself before you've even gotten it home. Simply let it lie peacefully—out of sight—until you reach your destination. Bear in mind also that carrying an uncaged reptile in public may even be illegal where you live.

Acclimatization

To most, the fact that a reptile's vivarium should be prepared *before the reptile's arrival* seems rather obvious, but too many people obtain a reptile first and wonder how and where they are going to keep it *afterward*. Do not be one of those people.

When you introduce your skink to its new home, do not simply empty it into the vivarium. The sudden shock of bright light and strange surroundings will cause it unnecessary stress. Instead, open the box or bag, place it on the floor of the vivarium, and allow your skink to come out when it's ready. It may appear immediately; if it doesn't, be patient. When it does at last emerge, it will almost certainly do one of two things: either explore its new surroundings,

Hissing can be a sign of a stressed skink—just give it time.

giving you the opportunity to watch its activities, or irritate you by vanishing into its hide.

Apart from removing soiled substrate, refreshing the drinking water, and offering food, you should not disturb your skink too much while it's getting used to you and its new environment. Acclimatization will take one to two weeks if the skink was bred and raised in captivity, but it can take as long as six to eight weeks if it was wild-caught or imported.

Once you see that your pet is no longer hiding, hissing, or displaying its tongue when you approach, you can start getting it used to being handled. Spend just brief periods with it at first—perhaps just a few minutes—and progressively lengthen the sessions over a week or two. Your skink will quickly come to recognize your scent and, if treated gently, feel safe and calm in your hands.

If your blue tongue is a captive-born juvenile or a healthy long-term captive, it should only require a couple of days to settle into its new home. Even though you will have a strong urge to handle it right away, give it time. Your patience will be rewarded with a happy, healthy, and friendly pet.

CHAPTER 5

Housing Your Skink

U nfortunately, you cannot give your pet lizard free run of your home, as you would a dog or a cat. Of course, some reptile species can be allowed out of their vivariums for short periods, provided that they are always watched closely. Left out for long periods of time, they could become chilled; entangle themselves in electrical cords, drapes, or other furnishings; or escape to the nearest crevice or hole, possibly never to be seen again. No, your reptile must have a cage of some kind—a vivarium, the purpose of which is not just to confine your pet but also to give it a secure environment in which it will remain healthy and feel at ease.

Building a Vivarium

Many of the commercially produced vivaria made today are truly wonderful pieces of furniture. They come in all

As long as your skink's needs are met, you can create your vivarium however you like.

shapes and sizes—wide, long, tall, angled, cornered, and round—and they can fit into just about any space. These superbly built structures are a joy to look at and would fit in with the decor of even the most discerning homeowner. Unfortunately, the majority cost hundreds or, in some cases, even thousands of dollars. So what is the alternative? Well, why not build one of your own?

Materials

There are no hard-and-fast rules as to how a vivarium should be built or what materials should be used. As long as your skink's needs—such as refuge, heat, light, and humidity—are met, everything else comes down to your own circumstances and personal preferences. For example, you'll need to take into account your budget, your available space, and whether you want a basic or natural setup. If expense is an issue, you can modify unused household items to suit your vivarium needs. Many very fine vivaria have been made from adapted cabinets, wardrobes, and shower units. Even large plastic storage bins can do the trick.

You can build your vivarium out of glass, wire, aluminum, melamine, glass fiber, metal, plastic, wood, or any combination of these materials. Whichever you decide

Vivarium furniture can be as cheap or as expensive as you want it to be. Buy a fancy hide at the pet store or recycle a large cardboard mailing tube—it's up to you.

to use, the vivarium should provide you with ease of access. In addition, it should be escape-proof, be free of sharp edges, be easy to clean, and be resistant to heat and humidity. Some materials are more suitable than others. Plastics and metals, for instance, are poor at retaining heat but can be used, for example, in a warm climate where artificial heat is unnecessary. Ventilation is practically nonexistent in all-glass aquaria, which are more suited to amphibians or fish; stale air will accumulate quickly inside them and affect the health of the reptile (unless you can either arrange some form of gentle and continuous airflow within them or remove the cover periodically so that fresh air can enter).

Melamine provides excellent insulation from temperature extremes as well as an easy-to-clean surface. If you want to use wood, marine plywood (used in boat building) is a good choice because it withstands both heat and moisture. To make the enclosure waterproof, use polyurethane paints or environmentally friendly wood preservatives. Allow two or three weeks with the vivarium's heat source turned on for them to cure and to dispel any odors, and then fill joints and small gaps with an animal-friendly (nontoxic) or aquarium sealant.

Orientation

Whether the end product opens from the top, side, or front will depend largely on where your lighting and heat fixtures will go. Keepers generally prefer vivariums that open from the front, with the front either glass or partially constructed of glass so that they can observe their skinks. Because the blue-tongued skink is usually fairly slow in its movements, cannot climb smooth vertical surfaces, and does not jump, an open-topped vivarium with lights and heat lamps suspended above it is also acceptable.

Ventilation

Insufficient airflow within the vivarium will cause a buildup of stale air, promote excessive humidity, and likely

One Skink at a Time

Seeing an animal enclosed on its own often distresses us because we imagine that it's missing contact with others of its own kind. But just as we humans sometimes prefer our own company, so too do many animals. Lizards (males in particular) are naturally solitary and territorial creatures. Although a blue-tongued skink's temperament is generally peaceful and easygoing, putting two or more together, especially in an artificial and restricted environment, can be disastrous. They may attempt to defend their individual and well-defined territories, sometimes resulting in vicious and even fatal fighting. Once a male has a grip on an opponent's flesh, he will often do a "crocodile roll," spinning their bodies over and lacerating his rival's body with his strong jaws. It's not uncommon for one or both parties to lose a limb during such fights. Even skinks that have lived together for a long time can suddenly turn on each other. It's important to house multiple skinks separately whenever possible.

cause the growth of harmful bacteria—all detrimental to your skink's health. To ventilate a completely enclosed vivarium, make two openings, each a minimum of 15.5 square inches (100 cm^2), one on each side of the vivarium, and cover them with a resilient, fine-mesh wire. Placing the holes some 4 to 6 inches (about 10 to 15 cm) above the vivarium floor will ensure that your skink is shielded against drafts. Because heat rises, side vents prevent the excessive heat loss that can occur when vents are located in a vivarium's ceiling.

Size

The blue-tongued skink is active and naturally inquisitive, so it needs ample room in which to move around and

The larger your vivarium, the more areas and furniture you can give your skink to explore.

explore its surroundings. The bigger the vivarium, the better. To keep just one skink requires a minimum floor area of 39 × 20 inches (100 × 50 cm), although 47 × 24 inches (120 × 60 cm) is better. Because this species cannot leap or climb, a minimum height of 15 inches (38 cm) is sufficient.

If you want to attempt breeding your skinks, then your female/male pair, or a trio of one male and two females, should be housed in a vivarium of no smaller than 59 × 24 inches (150 × 60 cm). Because each skink prefers to have its own territory within the vivarium—and allowing for a water bowl, a basking spot, and one or more hiding places—you'll need a floor area of at least 21.5 square feet (2 m²). Remember, it is always a good idea to have a spare vivarium handy in case of an emergency—such as an outbreak of hostilities (see "One Skink at a Time" on page 53).

Outdoor Enclosures

If you are fortunate to live in a climate that is warm for most, if not all, of the year, you can house your pet skink in

Don't be afraid to give your skink a little time outside—supervised, of course.

an outside enclosure during the warm periods. An outdoor enclosure will allow the skink access to beneficial fresh air and natural sunlight.

An open-air enclosure can be almost any size and shape you like, but it must always have a sufficiently high concrete, brick, or wooden wall surrounding it so that your skink cannot escape; adequate shelter for when the sun is at its strongest; and good drainage. In addition, the entire structure should be covered with strong chicken wire to keep out predators.

Substrates

In a very basic arrangement, the floor can be left bare, although it will require more frequent cleaning and sterilizing. You can use various materials, both natural and man-made, as a floor covering in your vivarium, but any substrate should be nontoxic and free from invertebrate pests and harmful bacteria. The substrate should also be simple to clean or replace and should not cause your skink irritation or discomfort. Try using newspaper, wood (such as aspen shavings, fir bark chips, or orchid bark chips), carpet, potting soil, smooth gravel, or sand.

Newspaper

Sheets of newspaper can be shaped to fit the vivarium's floor and weighted down with a few stones or heavy pieces of wood or bark. This is an ideal substrate because it's absorbent and moderately germ-free; it's inexpensive and readily available, and it can be replaced swiftly and effortlessly as soon as it becomes wet or dirty. In addition, newspaper is particularly useful in the housing of juvenile skinks, which defecate often.

Wood/Bark

If you want to replicate a dry woodland habitat in your vivarium, wood shavings or bark chippings make very pleasing and realistic substrates. Your skink's feces will adhere to these shavings or chips, clumps of which can then be easily scooped from the vivarium's floor. Aspen wood is especially suitable because it not only absorbs both dampness and odor but also is very easy to keep clean.

Wood shavings absorb dampness and odor and are very easy to clean up.

You'll find two different types of aspen wood: shredded and shavings (larger pieces). Buy shavings whenever possible because your skink could accidentally ingest the smaller pieces of shredded wood while trying to eat its food.

While some wood substrates work very well for skinks, you'll need to avoid a few others. Never use sawdust because your skink could inhale it, potentially resulting in respiratory problems. Also be careful to avoid shavings and chippings from cedars and pines—they can become poisonous when damp and could cause health problems if your skink ingests them.

Carpet

A range of domestic floor coverings can be adapted for use by reptile keepers. Carpet tiles, for instance, come in a variety of natural-looking colors and sizes and are easy to clean. Synthetic grass, also known as Astroturf, provides an excellent substitute for the real thing (singe the edges beforehand to prevent fraying). Although these materials can be comparatively expensive, they are long lasting and look attractive. As with newspaper, however, both carpet tiles and artificial grass need to be weighted down in some way to prevent your skink from working itself underneath the flooring.

If you use potting soil, make sure to keep it slightly damp to avoid it becoming dusty and harming your skink.

Soil

Potting soil—the kind that comes in sealed plastic bags—is usually sterile, free of fertilizer and invertebrate pests, and attractive in the vivarium. When fresh and very slightly damp, it looks almost black and can really show off your blue-tongued skink's colors. Unless sprayed with water or replaced regularly, however, potting soil dries out and becomes very dusty. Consequently, it could be damaging to the skink's health in the long term.

Using the regular soil from your garden or nearby countryside is definitely *not* recommended. It will likely be full of unwelcome invertebrates of many kinds, which will soon develop and reproduce in the heat and humidity of your vivarium.

Keep your blue tongue's comfort in mind and buy gravel with softer edges.

Coarse nontoxic sand is great for creating a desert landscape in your vivarium.

Gravel

Gravel, particularly that used in horticulture, can be a successful substrate for the vivarium. It is aesthetically pleasing, is easily managed, and comes in a variety of sizes and colors. Avoid the sharper types, which could cause your skink discomfort, and thoroughly wash all gravel—including the so-called prewashed kind—before its first use.

Sand

Some keepers of blue-tongued skinks use sand as a substrate in their vivaria, but you need to be careful about which kind you use. Very fine sand can work itself into a skink's belly scales or get into its eyes and nostrils, so choose a coarse type of sand. Also avoid the type of sand used in construction because it may be contaminated with caustic lyes and cement powder or contain sharp silica grains, which can cause problems if your pet ingests them. Play sand, available

A vivarium isn't complete without those fundamental items that keep your skink going plus a few creature comforts. From essentials, such as water and heating, to the things that provide a sense of security, such as hides, the following items will make your skink feel right at home.

Water Bowl

Some blue-tongued skinks will drink water readily while others will not, getting most of the fluids they require from the food that they eat. Nevertheless, a vessel of water should

Water should be available at all times, and the container it's in should be big enough to accommodate the skink should it decide to take a bath.

be available in your pet's vivarium at all times. The presence of water will serve three purposes: it will ensure that your skink always has something to drink, it will provide a place for bathing, and it will help maintain humidity within the vivarium to a certain degree.

The water bowl should be sturdy enough to prevent your skink from turning it over. For example, you can use a ceramic bowl, such as the kind made for feeding rabbits. The bowl should ideally be large enough for your skink to stretch out in from time to time. Blue-tongues like to immerse themselves, particularly just before sloughing. With this in mind, you should ensure that the water level will allow your skink to soak itself (head above water) without causing the water to overflow and flood the vivarium floor.

A well-placed log or carefully positioned rock will enable your skink to enter and exit the water bowl easily. If you can't fit a large enough water bowl in your vivarium, then provide just a smaller one for your skink to drink from and be prepared to either frequently spray your pet prior to sloughing or allow it to soak in a container outside of its vivarium.

Bear in mind that your skink will very likely defecate in its water container from time to time, so check it regularly. Even if it hasn't been soiled, you should still change the water at least every two days to keep it fresh.

Lighting

Research has clearly demonstrated that the majority of captive reptiles, diurnal species (active in daylight) in particular, that are deprived of natural sunlight derive many benefits from a simulated full-spectrum light source containing beneficial ultraviolet (UV). When regularly exposed to such illumination, skinks display a striking improvement in their health, disposition, activity level, and coloration. If you want a happy, healthy skink, your vivarium should include full-spectrum lighting.

Choosing the correct UV lighting is important for your skink's well-being. Lighting equipment produced especially for

The lighting you use can affect your skink's health, so use UV lights specifically made for reptiles.

captive reptiles is constantly being improved upon, and new products appear on the market on a fairly regular basis. Broad- or full-spectrum lighting is available in the form of lamps and tubes (which come in different lengths) from major pet-supply stores and dealers of specialty reptile products.

The majority of these lights emit the beneficial UVA rays that help encourage natural behavior and, more importantly, the UVB rays that stimulate the metabolism of dietary calcium and the production of vitamin D_3 in the skin. Your skink needs exposure to UVB light for only a few hours each day. Read product labels carefully to make sure that what you buy emits UVB.

UV lights come in three different strengths: 5 percent, 7 percent, and 10 percent. Mercury-vapor lamps and sunlamps provide ample UVB as well as heat and will benefit your skink. Don't hesitate to ask your dealer which lights are best suited to your purposes.

A good setup includes a suitably sized 5-percent UVB fluorescent tube in an aluminum reflector on the ceiling of the vivarium. Position the light where the skink can bask about 12 inches (30 cm) beneath it; the farther the distance between the light source and your lizard, the fewer the benefits. If your vivarium is taller than 20 inches (50 cm), you might need a light with a stronger UV output percentage.

If the climate where you live allows it, you can pen your blue-tongued skink outside on warm days, giving it access to both natural sunlight and fresh air. Make sure that it has shelter if the sun gets too strong, and cover the whole structure with strong wire mesh to keep out predators and prevent your skink from escaping.

Never, under any circumstances, place your vivarium by a window where it can catch the direct rays of the sun. Because glass filters out the ultraviolet part of the spectrum, your skink would gain no benefits from the light, and the vivarium would quickly overheat and roast your pet.

Turn off all bright lights in your skink's vivarium at night; a low-powered red light will let you see your lizard without disturbing it. With the help of a timer, you can tune the amount of natural light that your skink receives to the cycle of sun and moon. Under such a schedule, your skink will experience roughly the same lengths of day and night as it would in the wild.

Heating

You will have to provide heat for your subtropical blue-tongued skink, particularly if you don't live in a temperate

Photoperiods

The phase of light and dark (day and night) in every twenty-four hours is known as a *photoperiod*. The response of organisms to the lengthening or shortening of daylight triggers such activities as hibernation, migration, breeding, and other seasonal activities. Controlling the photoperiods of captive reptiles and amphibians is often an essential factor in their successful breeding.

climate. How you choose to heat the vivarium will depend, for the most part, on the vivarium's size, the materials used in its construction, and your preferences and circumstances.

Just as with lighting equipment, heating products—especially for the reptile hobbyist—are constantly being developed and improved upon. You can position heat pads or tubular greenhouse heaters beneath the floor of the vivarium. You can place heat tapes under the vivarium's floor or attach them to the exterior of the back or sides of the vivarium. If you prefer, you can suspend one or more ceramic heaters, infrared lamps, or tungsten lightbulbs either from the vivarium's ceiling or above an opening in

Temperature Gradient

However you decide to heat your vivarium, try to provide a temperature gradient so that your skink can move to and from a cooler spot if and when it wants to. Such an indispensable gradient is fairly easily attained by positioning a heating device, such as a heating pad, beneath the vivarium at one end, and an overhead thermostatically controlled radiant heat source, such as a spotlight, at the same end. During the day, the air temperature should be in the range of 86°F–95°F (30°C–35°C) at one end, and three to four degrees lower at the other end. A slight drop at night of five degrees or so is beneficial if you can do it, but temperatures should not be allowed to fall much below 70°F–75°F (21°C–24°C).

An ideal substrate temperature is around 95°F (35°C) at one end of the vivarium and around 86°F (30°C) at the other. This substrate temperature can also be allowed to fall at night to around 72°F (22°C). The larger your vivarium, the easier it will be for you to achieve this temperature variation.

Blue tongues are used to very warm environments, so heat lamps are important in mimicking their natural habitat.

the top of the vivarium. For a large vivarium, a combination of suspended heaters and pads may work best.

If you don't want th unattractive sight of heaters and their accompanying cables, thermostats, thermometers, switches, and plugs, you can keep your skink's vivarium in a "hot room." This is essentially a spare room or outbuilding that is heated to the required temperature by central heating or some form of heat-emitting device.

Whether you suspend your heater from or above the vivarium's ceiling or place it below the vivarium, it should be at a safe distance to prevent the structure, substrate, decorations, and of course your skink from burning. To be on the safe side, get the heating figured out a week or two before you introduce your skink to its new home. Find the right temperature by testing heaters at different settings and in different positions, sustain it with a thermostat set just above floor level, and monitor it with a thermometer.

Humidity

Humidity in an open-topped enclosure will be virtually nonexistent, but in a closed vivarium, the evaporation of

Hides are an important element of the vivarium—they give your blue tongue not only a place to sleep but also a place to retreat to when feeling insecure.

water from your skink's water bowl should produce enough humidity. The level of humidity in your skink's vivarium should be in the range of 20 to 45 percent. You can add moisture by moving the bowl closer to the heat source but still at a safe distance for your skink to drink and bathe comfortably. If condensation accumulates on the inside

Two Hides Are Better

If at all possible, equip your vivarium with two hides. Position one in the part of your vivarium with the higher temperature and the other in the area with the lower temperature. This arrangement will enable your pet to wander between the two of them so that it can self-regulate its body temperature and, in so doing, reduce the amount of stress that it might otherwise be subjected to. If you have multiple skinks in a single vivarium, provide an adequate number of hides so that each can choose which one it wants to shelter in or share.

of the vivarium walls, the humidity is too high; reduce it by moving the water farther from the heater or making bigger air vents. You might want to consider purchasing a hygrometer (a device that measures levels of humidity).

Hides and Other Furnishings

A sheltered hide that is large enough for the lizard to completely conceal itself in is one of the most important vivarium fixtures you can provide for your blue-tongued skink. A hide is some form of cover under or into which your skink can retreat and feel secure. It can be something as simple as a suitably sized plastic or earthenware drainage

While skinks don't really *climb*, they do enjoy clambering.

pipe, a cardboard mailing tube of appropriate diameter, half of a flowerpot positioned on its side, or any other safe, nontoxic household item that will provide your skink with a dark place it can use as a hideaway.

You can make your skink's hide a little more realistic looking and aesthetically pleasing by using a decorative hollow log or an arrangement of cork bark, rocks, or something similar. If you use rocks or heavy stones, make sure that they are stable and will not trap or crush your skink should it attempt to dig beneath them.

Because the blue tongue is a ground-dwelling lizard and does not climb, it does not need any branches in its vivarium, and it will trample, unearth, or devour any living plants. On the other hand, artificial plants and vines made of tough plastic or durable, easily washed fabric—can look very nice and survive a little trampling. You can even suspend them from the vivarium's ceiling or position them to hide from view vents, cords, thermostats, thermometers, your lizard's water bowl, and unsightly corners for a better aesthetic, if that's a concern for you.

Human Hygiene

Although most reptile diseases cannot be transmitted to humans, salmonella exposure is a problem. Salmonellosis is a common communicable disease occurring in reptiles, especially snakes and chelonians. The infection is caused by bacteria of the genus *Salmonella* and often causes illness in humans who have been careless in their hygiene practices following contact with an infected reptile. While maintaining strict cleaning procedures easily controls salmonella, all reptile owners still need to be vigilant. Consequently, always wash your hands thoroughly and use an antibacterial hand gel after handling your skink or the contents of its vivarium.

Although the blue-tongued skink, with its tiny legs and feet, is obviously not built for climbing, it still enjoys clambering over and exploring things. It's a good idea to provide one or two sturdy logs or perhaps a rock formation for your inquisitive pet. If such a feature is placed beneath your light source, your skink may even use it as a basking spot.

Routine Maintenance

Your vivarium should always be sanitary, not only for your skink but also for yourself, so begin a cleaning routine right away. Check the vivarium daily, removing uneaten food, excrement, and soiled substrate as soon as it appears. Replace your skink's water at least every other day, more often of course if it becomes dirty. Many reptiles have a frustrating habit of fouling their water as soon as it has been changed, and blue tongues are no exception, so check it again a couple of hours after replacing it.

Once every three or four months, completely empty the vivarium of all of its contents, put on rubber gloves, and give it a thorough scrubdown—paying particular attention to all corners and crevices—with a nontoxic disinfectant. Antiseptic vivarium cleaners are available specifically for the reptile keeper, but certain domestic cleaning fluids (kitchen cleaners, for example) work just as well. In the case of the latter, always read the label to ensure that they are animal friendly. While you are cleaning, keep your skink in a securely closed cloth bag in a warm place, or, if you have one, in a spare vivarium.

After scrupulously disinfecting the vivarium, rinse it at least twice and leave it to dry prior to cleaning any glass surfaces both inside and out. Thoroughly cleanse or change the substrate and disinfect, wash, dry, and replace all the furnishings before returning your skink to its home.

When you're all done, wash and sterilize any brushes, sponges, cloths, gloves, and other utensils that you used. After all, washing a dirty vivarium with a dirty sponge won't get you very far.

CHAPTER 6

Handling Your Skink

When handling your blue-tongued skink, always remember that being clutched and suddenly lifted off the ground is a totally foreign concept to reptiles. You'll need to handle your skink gently and with compassion. No two skinks are alike, and while some seem to enjoy the experience of being handled, others may try to escape your grasp or will have a negative reaction, such as not eating, after handling. Normally, the larger the lizard, the quicker it is to calm down. This chapter will help you learn when and how to handle your skink or allow others to do so.

Handle with Care

Lift your skink by gently putting one hand around its body, midway between its front and rear legs, and let it sit in your

When handling your skink, remember to support it completely. One way of doing this is to sit down and hold it on your lap.

palm while you support its tail with your other hand. Never hesitate when picking up your skink. A large hand hovering uncertainly overhead is just asking to be bitten.

To hold a full-grown adult skink, gently encircle its neck with your thumb and forefinger and let it lie on your forearm. A baby or sub-adult will usually be content with sitting in cupped hands.

Always support your skink completely and never allow it to fall from your grasp. Unlike iguanas, for example, skinks do not have the long limbs or claws necessary for climbing, so taking risks such as allowing your skink to sit on your shoulder while you walk around is asking for trouble. When you handle your pet, hold it no more than a few inches above a soft surface or your lap so that, should it fall, it will fall only a short distance and land on something forgiving. This tactic keeps injuries and expensive vet bills at bay.

Watch the Teeth

Biting comes naturally to lizards, which use their mouths in defense, in aggression, and to catch and devour their prey. However, blue tongues are also very curious and docile. The majority tame easily and quickly and are generally unwilling

Although these teeth don't look like much, keep in mind that they can help your blue tongue devour live food.

to bite, though some may do so when provoked. Normally, though, they prefer to adopt the characteristic curled defensive position, accompanied by hissing, tail flicking, and lunging.

Watch out for your skink's teeth during feedings. Food excites blue tongues, and yours may mistake a tasty-smelling finger for something edible. Don't handle food before picking up your skink or otherwise putting your hand inside the vivarium while your skink is in it.

Blue tongues have numerous small teeth on both their upper and lower jaws. Even a nip from a baby skink—though it won't necessarily draw blood—can be painful, and a bite from an adult can result in superficial lacerations. While bites from herbivorous lizards do not usually cause problems, those from carnivorous ones often can. Because the blue tongue's diet includes animal matter, its teeth are frequently laden with harmful bacteria that could cause the site of a bite to become infected. In the event of an accidental bite from your skink, always immediately wash the area and treat it with an antiseptic.

Consider the Claws

Your skink's teeth aren't your only concern. While a blue tongue's small claws won't damage an adult human's skin, they may scratch—albeit slightly and certainly never on purpose—the hands of a small child. To a child (or anyone not accustomed to skinks), the unexpected feeling

While a skink's claws might not bother you, children might be alarmed by an unintentional scratch.

of claws on skin can be both startling and unsettling. Always supervise children and apprehensive handlers at all times, particularly if it's someone's first time handling a skink.

Be Aware of Bathroom Habits

Like all animals, skinks need to rid themselves of bodily waste every now and then. Unless it has an upset stomach, a blue-tongued skink will normally defecate and urinate once a day. Because skinks spend long periods being still, they tend to do their business when active—or handled.

A skink's urine is a clear, odorless fluid, but its solid waste does have a slight odor. Neither product will stain clothes, and you can easily clean yourself up. A skink suddenly using its handler as a toilet may take the person by surprise, sometimes causing him or her to drop the animal or knock it off his or her lap. Thus, if a friend or child wants to handle your skink, warn the person first about what *might* happen so that he or she will not be startled if it does. You can often prevent such accidents by simply allowing your skink to walk around on some newspaper for a short time

As with any small animal, know that there's a chance your blue tongue might "have an accident" while being held.

before being handled. That way, it can do its business on the paper and not on your hand.

Be Careful of the Tail

Unlike some lizard species, the blue-tongued skink does not drop its tail (a defense mechanism that allows part of the tail to separate from the lizard's body, allowing the lizard to escape a predator). Nevertheless, the skink's tail can still break off if trapped or pulled hard. A lost tail will never grow back completely. Although you should accustom your skink to having its tail touched, never pick it up by this appendage, especially if the rest of its body is unsupported.

When to Leave It Alone

You will quickly come to recognize your skink's disposition, which, as with all animals, can change from time to time and in varying circumstances. Eventually, you'll be able to judge when you should and when you should not handle it.

Be gentle when handling your skink's tail—if tugged hard enough, it may come off, and it won't ever grow back fully.

If little ones want to interact with your pet blue tongue, hold the skink yourself so that they can do so without harming it.

Generally speaking, you shouldn't handle your skink while it's shedding its skin. Many reptile species are inclined to be irritable, withdrawn, and reluctant to eat during this process, and your skink may not appreciate being handled while it's feeling this way. In addition, handling might force some of the skin to slough off before it is ready, possibly causing problems, such as scarring or infection, later.

Another time to leave your skink alone is during mating and gestation. When breeding skinks, it's best to minimize handling so that the animals will behave as naturally and unhindered as possible. If, during the breeding season, you need to move specimens (for vivarium maintenance, for example), do so by encouraging the skinks to first crawl into a bag or box. Then you can remove the bag or box to a warm and safe place without actively handling the skinks themselves. Leave them in the bag or box until you have done whatever was necessary, and then put it back in the vivarium and allow them to emerge when they are ready.

CHAPTER 7

Feeding Your Skink

The blue-tongued skink is omnivorous, meaning that it will eat a variety of foodstuffs in captivity from flower heads to fruit, berries to beetles, and vegetables to venison. Because of this, feeding your wonderful and endearing reptile could not be easier. You'll just need to keep certain important factors—when and how much to feed, what kind of supplements to add and when, what foods are unsafe for your skink, and so on—in mind.

When to Feed Your Skink

While you should never leave your adult skink without food for more than a few days, you shouldn't feed it every day either. Feeding adults on alternate days is a good system. You may find that your pet prefers to feed more or less often. Generally, neonates (babies), juveniles, and sub-adults (fully grown but sexually immature skinks under twelve months) should be fed every day, or at least five days a week. Because

Fruits and vegetables will make up most of your blue tongue's diet—about 70 percent of it.

this species is diurnal, you should obviously offer it food during the day, while it's awake.

Avoid, when possible, offering food to your skink in the late afternoon or evening. It may not be able to properly digest anything eaten at these times, when the temperatures in its vivarium fall to their nighttime settings. Likewise, if you choose to feed in the morning, wait an hour or so for your skink to become sufficiently alert before you offer it food.

What to Feed to Your Skink

Having a variety of the right foodstuffs is the key to a healthy blue-tongued skink. A skink's diet should consist of about 50 percent vegetables and greens; 30 percent animal protein in the form of meat, fish, invertebrates, and rodents; and 20 percent fruits and flowers. Feeding any pet is an interesting and fun experience because you get to discover its likes and dislikes, and also if it is a fussy nibbler or a greedy glutton. Below are some food suggestions for your skink. Experiment!

Vegetarian Fare

The bulk of a blue-tongued skink's diet should consist of vegetables, such as carrot (grated), prickly-pear pad, fresh corn and okra, and the greens of such things as kale,

Frozen Vegetables

For the sake of convenience, many people purchase frozen vegetable mixes for their reptiles, defrosting portions for feedings. However, you should use frozen vegetables only *occasionally* because feeding them on a regular basis can lead to a thiamine deficiency, which can cause disorders of the central nervous system. (Thiamine forms part of the vitamin B complex and is essential for carbohydrate metabolism and converting various nutrients and acids into fats and proteins.) So, try to give your skink fresh food more often than not.

Balanced Nutrition

Your skink requires a balanced diet to stay healthy. Calcium and phosphorus are essential elements, playing an important role in the lizard's utilization of carbohydrates and fats, the synthesis of protein for the growth and repair of cells and tissues, the building of strong bones and teeth, and the functioning of organs such as the heart and kidneys. Both of these elements are found in many greens and vegetables such as squash, endive, escarole, dandelion, mustard, and turnip greens, and in fruits such as mango, fig, banana, papaya, and raspberry. As long as you regularly give some of these to your skink—together with the occasional small mouse, a locust or two, and a little meat—you'll have a healthy and content reptile.

cabbage, sprout, green beans, turnip, beet, collard, endive, mustard, parsley, romaine, escarole, pea pods, squash, and celery. The remainder of its diet should be made up of fruit and animal protein.

A variety of fresh calcium-rich fruits and flowers—such as those of nasturtium, rose, strawberry, raspberry, blueberry, and fig—can make up the remainder of the vegetarian portion of your skink's diet. You can add to these smaller amounts of banana, peach, pear, plum, and cranberry. Blue tongues as a species seem to love fruit more than anything, with bananas, pears, and strawberries being particular favorites. Chopped apples, tomatoes, and grapes are also devoured enthusiastically, as are blackberries, cucumbers, and melons. Other foodstuffs that are high in fiber and have a suitable ratio of calcium and phosphorus include hibiscus and dandelion flowers and leaves, broccoli stalks and leaves, and mulberry leaves.

As you can see, the list of vegetables, fruits, and flowers that you can offer your blue-tongued skink is almost endless. You'll find a few exceptions, however. Avoid rhubarb and avocado, which are toxic to many lizard species; spinach, which neutralizes the positive effects of calcium; most varieties of lettuce, which—although skinks like them—have almost no nutritional value; and citrus fruits such as oranges, lemons, and limes, which are acidic and can cause diarrhea in your pet. Otherwise, experiment with a variety of produce and visit local markets that have interesting choices (Asian markets are excellent for healthy options such as bok choy, mustard, and peavine greens). Always wash and rinse all vegetables and fruit well to remove any harmful contaminants.

Meatier Options

Blue tongues also enjoy a variety of meats. You'll find plenty of debate about whether to feed captive animals—regardless of species—raw or cooked meat. Obviously, animals in the wild do not cook their meat (or fish, or anything else for that matter) before they eat it. But that doesn't mean that you can't or shouldn't feed your skink cooked food. A lot of lizard keepers have, for many years (and apparently successfully) given their pets cooked chicken, turkey, beef, ham, and other such meats. Is this good for your skink, or is it unnatural? No one seems to have the answer. So, if you prefer to feed cooked meat and your skink seems to be thriving on it, then continue to offer it.

If, however, you prefer to give your lizard raw meat, then beef heart and lamb heart are excellent options. They

Meat should make up 30 percent of your skink's diet.

contain little fat, are easy to find and inexpensive, and can be cut into suitably sized pieces and kept in the freezer. (Always allow frozen meat to thaw thoroughly prior to feeding.) Blue-tongued skinks will also enjoy fish occasionally, as well as low-fat, high-quality canned dog or cat food, which provide the added health benefit of their vitamin and mineral content.

How to Feed Your Skink

Quoting the precise amount of food that your blue-tongued skink will require at each feeding may depend upon its age, vivarium size, and activity level (the larger the vivarium, the more active the skink and the more food it will need). You'll also have to consider special circumstances such as whether your skink is about to slough its skin, mate, or give birth.

As a general rule, offer adult skinks fresh food on alternate days. Offer babies and younger skinks food as wanted—in other words, however much they will eat and whenever they will eat it—daily over a six-day period, letting them fast on the seventh day. Decrease this frequency to alternate days, or even less depending upon your young skinks' particular preferences and requirements, as they grow.

In order to establish your pet skink's needs, give it what you think is a suitable quantity of mixed plant, vegetable, and animal matter. If it eats everything fairly quickly, offer it more in small increments until it stops showing interest. Do the same at subsequent feeds, and you will soon ascertain how much

Because you'll be feeding your skink very fresh food, you'll want to remove it if it goes uneaten for a few hours.

food it needs. Remove uneaten food after a few hours or it will soon dry out in the heat of the vivarium and start to smell.

Place the food in a shallow but heavy dish (shallow enough to allow your skink access and heavy enough to prevent it from tipping over while the skink feeds). Always remove the food dish and wash it well after your skink finishes eating. Use this dish solely for your skink's food and keep it separate from your own tableware. Removing the food bowl after each feeding will not only help keep the vivarium clean but will also enable you to see how much your skink ate and help you determine what it needs at the next feeding.

Supplements

In its natural habitat, the blue-tongued skink devours a variety of flowers, fruit, vegetation, and small animals. With the additional benefit of unfiltered sunlight, it receives all of the balanced nutrients essential for its good health. In captivity, however, you'll need to supplement your skink's diet to keep your pet strong and healthy. You'll find several tried-and-true supplements for your blue-tongued skink, including both manufactured and natural sources.

Vitamins and Minerals

Manufactured dietary supplements usually come in two basic forms: liquid and powder. With the liquid, you usually add a few drops to the lizard's drinking water. This is fine for baby skinks, which should have a smaller, shallower drinking vessel, but an adult's large water container may dilute the supplement to the point of negating its benefit.

You'll be able to purchase good powdered supplements from most large pet-supply stores, reptile breeders, and your vet, the latter of whom will also be able to advise you on its use. A dietary mineral supplement should contain phosphorus-free calcium and vitamin D_3, which is essential if you are unable to give your skink full-spectrum lighting and it does not have regular access to natural unfiltered sunlight. Dust the food lightly with the supplement at each feeding. Also lightly dust the food with a multivitamin supplement weekly for mature

If your blue tongue doesn't have regular access to sunlight or full-spectrum lighting, give it a vitamin D supplement.

nonbreeding adults and two or three times a week for babies, sub-adults, mating pairs, and females carrying young.

Cod-liver oil is another good supplement for skinks as it contains vitamins A and D and is excellent for your pet's skin, joints, and immune system. Add three or four drops to your skink's food once or twice a week (be warned: too much can give it diarrhea).

Just as a vitamin/mineral deficiency can result in a skink's poor health, so too can an overload—so do not be overzealous in supplementing. If you are in doubt as to the quantity and type of vitamin and/or mineral supplements to give your pet lizard, consult with your veterinarian.

Rodents

You can also supplement your skink's diet with baby rats and mice; the bones in the rodents' bodies provide vital calcium. Blue tongues seem to prefer baby rats to baby mice. Whether the rodents are alive or dead will make no difference to your skink. If you prefer to purchase prekilled rodents, they will almost certainly be frozen. This means, of course, that you will need to keep them in your own freezer until you feed them to your skink, and you will also have to make sure that they are completely thawed when you use them. If rodents are difficult to obtain, you can instead sprinkle your skink's meat or fruit with a liberal amount of grated cuttlefish bone or bonemeal.

Crickets are more than a meal—all of their jumping around gives your blue tongue a chance to get some exercise.

Insects

Introducing a handful of larger insects—giant mealworms, crickets, waxworms, locusts, and so on—into the vivarium every now and then is a good idea. The insects will usually quickly seek out hiding places or fly or jump around, thereby enabling the skink to spend some time actively hunting and catching its food. Make sure you gut-load the insects twenty-four to forty-eight hours before you give them to your skink (see the sidebar "Gut-Loading Insects" on page 85).

If you find that commercially available insects are difficult to obtain where you live or are too expensive, collecting your own from the wild can save you money and be an interesting pastime in itself. If you choose this option, disregard tiny insects, such as termites and ants, because your skink will ignore them and they will either die or escape into your home. Also rule out flying species, such as moths and butterflies, which will either alight on the vivarium's ceiling (out of your skink's reach) or fly out of it altogether. Instead, concentrate your efforts on insects such as caterpillars, grasshoppers, crickets, and beetles.

You can attract many insects, including beetles and crickets, at night to a bright light illuminating a white sheet; pick up the larger ones as they land on the sheet. *Beating* and *sweeping* are two other proven methods of catching insects. Beating is used to find insects that live in trees and shrubs. All you will need here is a sturdy stick and something in which to catch the insects; a white sheet laid on the ground or an upturned umbrella will suffice. You then simply give a branch a good thwack with the stick to dislodge any invertebrates dwelling in its foliage. This method is very good for obtaining caterpillars, and beetles and other leaf-eaters can also be found this way. Sweeping entails sweeping a net from side to side in front of you as you walk in tall grass and low vegetation and is a good method for obtaining grasshoppers and crickets.

If you harvest your insects from the wild, do not take them from areas that have been sprayed with insecticides or herbicides. In addition, avoid heavily populated urban areas, never take more insects than you need at any one time, and always remember that, in certain areas, some insect species may be protected by law.

Snails

Most members of the genus *Tiliqua* have a particular liking for snails. As a consequence, many owners of blue-tongued skinks like to give their pets snails that they've found in the garden, in ponds and streams, and elsewhere. There are, however, concerns over whether this is a good idea because certain species of snail carry parasitic flatworms (*Trematoda*).

While snails are not essential to your skink's diet, their shells are an excellent source of calcium. If you want to give your pet wild snails, you have to "detox" them first. Put them in a clean plastic container with some lettuce leaves and a little water, cover the container, and leave them for three or four days. In that time, they will either purge themselves of any toxins or die from them. If the snails are still alive at the end of the detox period, it is safe to feed them to your skink.

An alternative method is to simply use snails produced for human consumption. These are bred and reared to the very highest standards. Whatever type of snails you offer to your skink, make sure that your pet eats them right away, or its vivarium will end up covered in slime trails.

Refusal to Eat

Very occasionally, a skink will completely refuse to eat, no matter what type of food is offered. This is natural during breeding time, in which case there is no cause for worry; your skink will resume feeding again once sexual activity has ceased. At other times, your skink may simply get bored with its food. Try tempting it with some different fruits and vegetables or colorful flowers (grate, shred, or chop these treats, as some blue tongues may go several days before realizing that the new food items are actually edible!). Rejection of food may, however, indicate a problem, such as an intestinal or mouth infection, which will need to be treated. If the skink is not breeding, continues refusing to eat for more than two weeks, and its condition starts to deteriorate, consult your veterinarian.

Gut-Loading Insects

Even though vegetables, fruit, and other organic matter form the larger part of its diet, the brown house cricket is an omnivorous scavenger, consuming just about anything it can get its jaws into, and it will damage upholstery, drapes, clothes, and carpeting if given the opportunity. When other food sources are not available, adult crickets will often devour their own young as well as weakened and recently dead adults. However, you must ensure that you give your crickets nutritious food so they pass that nourishment onto your pet skink. This procedure is commonly known as gut-loading.

Rolled oats, crushed dog biscuit, chicken meal, or a mixture of these or similar foods, placed in a shallow dish with the occasional slice of fresh fruit or vegetable such as carrot or potato, will provide an extremely good-quality diet for your crickets. Commercially prepared, high-calcium insect foods are also available and worth considering as an alternative. Once you're ready to feed your skink, you can dust the crickets with a mineral supplement powder to guarantee that your pet will receive the comprehensive nutrition it requires.

CHAPTER 8

Breeding Your Skink

To witness the animals you have cared for, sometimes for several years, produce young is extremely rewarding. Because many species of reptile are reluctant to breed in captivity unless they are healthy and at ease in their surroundings, successful results are a reasonably reliable indication that the husbandry is satisfactory and they are comfortable and free of stress. Breeding your pet can also have financial benefits if you choose to sell the offspring. A young blue-tongued skink can demand over a hundred dollars, so a litter of half a dozen or more can easily cover any skink-related expenses you have incurred over the past year or two. One note: if you do choose to breed, do so responsibly and with counsel from someone with experience breeding skinks.

Sexing

If you're happy to keep just the one skink, then whether it is a male or female will make little difference to you. When kept in isolation, the sexes demonstrate no difference in temperament, and both make equally good pets. Only if you intend to breed, and therefore keep two or three together, will sexing them become necessary.

Because the sexes display so little difference between them, establishing whether an individual blue tongue is male or female can be difficult. In some cases, it can prove virtually impossible—particularly when they are sub-adults. You'll find all sorts of methods for distinguishing males from females, but to do it with any accuracy often requires you to utilize more than one of them.

Visual Inspection

Across the center of the body, between the fore- and hind legs, male blue-tongued skinks are frequently rectangular

Female blue tongues tend to be slightly longer than their male counterparts.

and females generally ovoid (egg-shaped). This is sometimes apparent just after they are born and again when they are adults. You'll always find exceptions to the rule, however, and an individual's weight will also have a bearing on how accurate this method of sexing is.

Generally speaking, adult males are usually of heavier build and possess bigger, broader heads. Compare the width of the skink's head with that of its body at its widest point, just in front of the hind legs. If its head is noticeably wider, the skink is, in all probability, male. If its head is the same width as or narrower than its body, the skink is most likely female. Males may also have slightly more pronounced markings. But, once again, there are exceptions in both cases.

Female blue tongues are inclined to have slightly longer bodies, which is clearly evident when you look at the distance between the front and hind legs and at the shape of the tail, which tends to taper to a point over a longer distance than in the male. However, you'll need to compare two or three skinks—preferably more—if this purely visual evaluation is to be of any value in sex determination.

One of the few dependable visual cues in determining sex in mature blue-tongued skinks is the occurrence or absence of seminal plugs. These are small, white, translucent wads of dried semen, approximately 1 inch (2.5 cm) in length, that adhere to the invaginated hemipenes (the *hemipenes* are the male copulatory organs) of some male lizards and snakes, proving that the reptile is reproductively active (producing sperm). A sexually active male will release these plugs, typically in pairs, often on a daily basis. They can also be observed when the hemipenes are everted when the lizard is excreting waste, but at that point there's little doubt as to the sex of the reptile.

Because seminal plugs frequently get lost among a vivarium's substrate, they are regularly ignored and discarded. This is especially the case if the vivarium floor is covered with leaves, bark chippings, or gravel. On a surface of sand, soil, Astroturf, or newspaper, however, seminal plugs become fairly evident but may be mistaken for the skink's normal waste products.

In a mature male blue-tongued skink, the hemipenes may appear in the form of a bulge protruding from either side of the base of the tail. Examine the underside of your skink and look at the cloacal flap, or vent. If there is a lump on either side of it and toward the tail, you could have a male.

Lastly, simply putting two adults together and watching them closely will often tell you all you need to know. A female confronted by a male will, for example, walk slowly with jerky movements and frequently start to whip her tail erratically from side to side in a snakelike way, eventually raising it as she signals she is ready to receive him. If a female comes face to face with another female, then (unless one or both have particularly aggressive temperaments) neither is likely to react to the other.

At a Glance

The state in which the sexes display noticeable differences in markings, coloration, and size or structure is known as *sexual dimorphism* and is apparent in numerous lizard species. Unfortunately, the blue-tongued skink is not one of them and lacks any clearly defined, totally foolproof characteristic pattern or color that could help determine its sex.

Males in the same confined area will probably act very aggressively toward each other. A male in the presence of a female may completely freeze his movements and look intently at her before lunging forward and gripping her on the neck with his jaws. Eventually, after maneuvering her into a suitable position, he may try to raise his tail beneath her, evert his copulatory organ, and attempt to mate.

Sexing Procedures

Hemipenile eversion, or *popping*, is sometimes successful in sexing neonates (newborns) and very young blue tongues. Turn the skink on its back and hold it ventral side up in one hand, circling the part of its body directly in front of the vent between your thumb and forefinger. Hold the skink's tail in the other hand and place your thumb on the base of the tail, a centimeter or two behind the vent, and smoothly roll your thumb toward the vent while applying delicate pressure. If the skink is male, the pressure will usually cause one or both of its hemipenes to evert, or *pop out*.

This procedure causes no distress to the skink if performed correctly, but the use of too much pressure can cause it injury. Always watch an experienced lizard keeper

The hemipenes are located on the male skink's ventral surface between its hind legs and the base of its tail.

do it first, or ask that person if he or she will do it for you if you have any doubts about doing it yourself.

Prerequisites for Successful Breeding

The blue-tongued skink, when kept in optimum conditions, will reach sexual maturity when just twelve months old. The male skink you intend to breed should be twelve months old or older, and the female should be at least two years old.

While the actual mating is up to your skinks, there are a few things you can do to help everything go smoothly. You'll need to prepare both the skinks and their vivarium. Be sure that you are feeding a balanced and well-supplemented diet to the skinks you intend to breed. In addition, they must be well matched in approximate size, weight, and health, and sexually mature (at least twelve months old). If the male and female have grown up together in the same vivarium, they should, if possible, be separated from each other for the length of the cooling period. This will usually renew their interest in each other for when they are reintroduced.

An Unsuccessful Probe

A method commonly used in the sexing of both lizards and snakes is cloacal probing. This procedure employs the use of a smooth, slender, tapered, and blunt instrument lubricated with a nonspermicidal fluid, such as tap water or sterile saline. You insert the probe into the reptile's cloaca (vent) and direct it toward the tip of the tail. The probe will generally slide a greater distance into a male reptile than into a female.

In the majority of lizard and snake species, the procedure works very well. Unfortunately, it is useless in the case of blue-tongued skinks because both sexes have similarly sized cloacal pockets. The probe will reach a comparable distance in all blue tongues, regardless of sex.

Cooling your skinks during their *brumation*, or winter period, is considered essential if they are to breed successfully. The process generally begins in November and lasts until March, although different time zones, climates, and environments should be taken into consideration when determining your own breeding methods.

A cooling period replicates the conditions your skinks would experience in the wild and can actually encourage courtship performance. Before you start cooling, first ensure that your skinks are in good health and have good fat reserves (full, heavy tails and firm, fleshy flanks).

You'll need to lower the temperature of the vivarium and shorten the lighting periods to mimic wintertime.

Two to three weeks prior to cooling, you'll wean your skinks completely off food so that their digestive tracts are emptied of any undigested matter, which would otherwise decompose in their stomachs in the colder temperatures. (**Note:** you should still provide clean, fresh water at all times.) Gradually lower the vivarium's temperature over a two- to three-week period to between 55F and 60F degrees (13C and 16°C). Simultaneously reduce the day length from twelve to ten hours, and finally to eight hours. Maintain these winter conditions for the next eight to twelve weeks. Do not feed or handle your skinks during this period, but check on them weekly to make sure they are not showing signs of illness. Some breeders like to place their skinks in small containers in a cellar or an outbuilding such as a garage with no light or heat for the entire cooling period. If you decide to do this, you won't have to worry about changing the temperature in your vivarium or reducing the day length. Just ensure that the temperature gets no lower than 40°F (5°C).

When you're ready to end the cooling period, gradually increase the temperature over ten to fourteen days to its previous summer settings. At the same time, offer small amounts of food. While females will usually resume feeding right away, males will often continue to fast for another four to six weeks until breeding has ended. If the male and female have been separated during the cooling period, let them have at least two feedings each before reintroducing them to each other.

Courtship and Mating

When you put your skinks together for mating, ensure that you have the time to watch the whole proceedings to make sure they don't get overly excited or aggressive and cause each other severe injury. If you leave them unattended, even for just a short while, you may return to find one has lost a foot or part of its tail.

As the female comes into season, the male will spend a lot of time following her around the vivarium. Occasionally, she will reject his advances and scurry away as soon as he gets within an inch of her. Eventually, however, she should submit. If she doesn't, try again two or three days later. If you still have no luck, you will either have to try her with another male or abandon breeding and try again next season.

Generally, the male grips the female in the area of her neck and attempts to position his tail beneath hers to align their vents, often while using one of his rear legs to scratch her on top of the base of her tail. In a submissive response,

A Little Mystery

You need to give your breeding pair time apart because familiarity acquired over the years can actually hinder mating. Separating and then reintroducing them two or three months later will add a certain freshness to their relationship and encourage copulation.

Male skinks often bite females during mating, which can sometimes lead to serious wounds.

the female will finally elevate her tail and allow copulation to take place.

In some cases, a male will become so enthusiastic that he will seize the female by the head, forelimb, or tail in what can only be described as a breeding fury. Do not get too worried at this point—the male should quickly find the correct embrace, and any lacerations suffered by the female should be minor and heal swiftly. On rare occasions, females can receive deep, bloody wounds during mating. In the majority of cases, these will heal fairly quickly and without any problems, though some scarring may remain. Keep the wounds clean.

Mating can last anywhere from 90 seconds to over an hour. When the pair separates and the female completely rejects any further advances from the male, mating is over. One mating is often sufficient for fertilization, although some skinks may choose to mate three or four times. No harm comes from allowing multiple matings unless the female looks weak or badly lacerated by the male's jaws.

Isolating the Female

As soon as mating is over, remove the female and place her in a vivarium of her own. This ensures that she's free from any further unwanted advances from the male and benefitting from all of the food given to her. Gravid (pregnant) females continue to eat throughout their gestation and must eat well for the developing embryos to receive the nourishment they need. It is a good idea to weigh the female prior to mating and then weigh her again periodically after breeding. If she starts to increase in weight, you can be almost certain she is gravid.

The gestation period of blue-tongued skinks can vary, depending on the species, from 90 to 170 days, throughout which the embryos develop inside the female in a primitive placenta. During this time, offer her sufficient food as well as an increased calcium supplement at alternate meals. Ensure that she has access to a basking spot of at least 95°F (35°C).

Keep the nursery vivarium as simple and as sterile as possible. Disinfect it prior to the female's introduction, and cover the floor with two or three sheets of newspaper. In addition, provide your skink with a hide box filled with shredded or crumpled paper. The water bowl should be shallow enough to allow baby skinks to climb out should they be born during the night or when you are not present and fall in while exploring their new surroundings.

The Importance of Nutrition

As already mentioned, it is critical to provide gestating females with sufficient food of sufficient variety along with the necessary vitamin and mineral supplements. Not doing so can result in birth defects such as no eyes, no lower jaw, a twisted spine, or a permanently curled tail. Taking good care of your female during gestation helps produce healthy, thriving offspring.

Birth and Development

Some gravid females swell to a huge extent, whereas others astonish even the most knowledgeable breeders with unanticipated young. As her time advances, however, the gravid female will often become more hostile, possibly rejecting food and seeming constantly agitated. In the latter stages, her breathing may also become labored as the babies press against her lungs and other internal organs.

As the birth of the young becomes imminent, the female will retreat into the hide box, where she will sometimes remain for several days. Immediately prior to giving birth (often in the early hours of the morning), she will usually pass a great deal of fluid, often saturating the floor of the vivarium in which she is housed. Look out for this: when it happens, birth of the young is literally minutes away.

Depending on the species, female blue-tongued skinks produce between four and twenty babies. Each baby is born in a transparent membrane from which it breaks out almost immediately. As the babies are born, their umbilical cords break off naturally, leaving just half an inch or so to shrivel and fall away in the following two or three days. Never try to

Most blue tongues give birth to between four and six live young.

95

These young Tanimbars look exactly like their parents, even at this young age.

speed up the process by pulling at an umbilical cord because this can result in bleeding and possibly lasting damage.

The adult female eats any unfertilized ova she may pass. Likewise, the babies eat their placentas, which are important first meals because they are full of the antibodies and vitamins essential for a good start in life.

Again depending on the species, some females produce small litters of comparatively large babies and others large litters of small babies. On average, baby blue-tongued skinks weigh around 0.35 ounces (10 g) and measure 5 inches (approximately 130 mm) in length. They can more than double in length in their first three months, with growth continuing at a rapid rate. Under favorable conditions, young skinks attain their full adult size in eighteen months.

Keep an eye on your female; adult female skinks can lose a lot of their body weight after giving birth. Your skink will need regular, nourishing feedings to help her weight return to normal as soon as possible. If you have been housing your pair of skinks together on a permanent basis, you can put them back together two or three weeks after the birth of the young, once the female has regained her strength and weight.

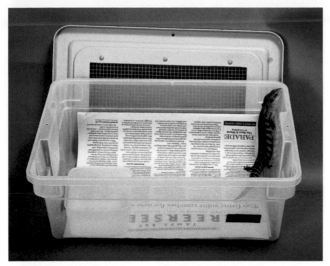

Small plastic tubs like this one make ideal temporary homes for baby blue tongues.

Rearing the Young

While baby blue tongues are miniatures of their parents in many ways, you will have to make some special considerations for them. Not only are you caring for infants, but you are also caring for many more skinks than you were before.

Housing

Once the female has delivered all her babies, you can remove her from the nursery vivarium and put her on her own to recover. The babies are completely independent as soon as they are born and, at the outset, can all share the same container, such as a 10-gallon aquarium. After six weeks or so, however, the skinks need to be separated from one another and housed individually. If you allow the baby skinks to stay together too long, they may fight, which can result in lacerations, broken limbs, severed tails, and nasty head wounds.

Plastic shoeboxes are ideal for housing individual baby skinks, and you can stack several inside a large vivarium. The air in the lower boxes will get refreshed every time you

Feed your baby skinks small mealworms and other insects that will fit into their mouths.

open them (when you feed the babies), so you don't have to worry about suffocation. When the babies are about three months, you can transfer them to larger plastic containers, where they can remain (unless you sell them off) until they are one year old.

Maintain the babies at the same temperature as the adults—but without the temperature reduction at night—and keep them on a simple newspaper substrate. This will prevent accidental ingestion of substrate such as loose bark or gravel, which could cause serious problems later.

Feeding

Baby skinks normally start eating two to three days after they are born and should be fed six of the seven days each week. Feed them the same food that you give the adults, but finely chop or grate it into manageable pieces. Remove any hard stalks and kernels, and dust the food well with a vitamin/mineral supplement.

In addition, make sure that any insects you give the babies are small enough to fit in their mouths. Small mealworms—particularly those that have just molted (these are paler in color)—small crickets, locust nymphs, and waxworms are good at the beginning, and you can progress to larger ones as the baby skinks grow. Provide water in shallow dishes. If the babies have not eaten after five days since birth, tweak the temperature and/or amount of light they are exposed to a little each day until you get results.

If you initially house the baby skinks together, do not offer them live food during its first few weeks. Jumping, running, or wriggling insects can get the babies excited at mealtimes, and they may mistake each other's tails and toes for dinner. Similarly, check regularly to see that none of the skinks is being a bully or eating more than its share. The bigger and more powerful of the group may take most of the food, resulting in their own quicker growth and the underdevelopment of the rest. If you don't yet want to give each skink its own container, you can simply take turns feeding each separately, either by hand or by removing each one and placing it, temporarily, with the food in a separate container.

Handling Babies

Baby blue-tongued skinks are generally quite spirited little lizards, and they will hiss and attempt to bite at your approach. This behavior is, of course, instinctive as a defense mechanism against possible predators in the wild. With regular, gentle handling, however, your skinks will quickly learn to trust you and settle down. (See chapter 6 for information on how to handle juvenile skinks.)

Gently handle your baby blue tongues on a regular basis to acclimate them to human touch.

CHAPTER 9

Your Skink's Health

No matter how meticulous you may be in trying to safeguard your blue-tongued skink, it may still become ill or injured at some point. Therefore, knowing the warning signs and what actions, if any, to take is immensely useful. You should be able to correct the problem yourself in many instances, but some ailments may require a veterinarian's attention.

Finding a Veterinarian

With proper care and attention, your blue-tongued skink should stay free from harm and illness throughout most of its life with you. Nonetheless, mishaps can occur, and sicknesses can develop quickly. Knowing that you have a fairly priced, experienced, dependable, and friendly vet not too far away will give you great peace of mind.

Unfortunately, finding a vet for a blue-tongued skink isn't as easy as finding one for cats and dogs.

They're Out There

Some reptile owners are surprised to learn that their pets might, at some stage, require veterinary attention. They mistakenly believe that vets treat only animals with fur and feathers and that they'll have to handle their exotic pets' illnesses or injuries alone. Nothing could be further from the truth.

The popularity of keeping exotic animals such as reptiles and amphibians is rapidly increasing, largely due to the comparatively little attention these amazing creatures require—a helpful attribute in this busy society of ours. Exotic pets also appeal to a different sensibility than their furry counterparts do. Illuminated in natural settings within their enclosures, these animals bring their keepers ever closer to nature and the wild. Because of this surge in popularity, veterinarians strive to stay up to date with reptilian trends and medicine. In addition, when you consider that some reptiles, particularly those with unusual colors or markings, can command hundreds of dollars, it is not so surprising that their owners have a vested interest in their health. These owners have created a demand for the very best veterinary care.

You should begin searching for a veterinarian before you've acquired your skink. Don't make the mistake of waiting until your reptile becomes injured or ill to find healthcare; in a hurry to get a diagnosis and treatment, you may not end up with the best care for your skink. Besides, you'll need a good vet because your skink will need a general exam and screening for internal parasites as soon as you bring it home.

Finding a veterinarian who has experience in handling and treating reptiles can be tricky; many treat mainly cats and dogs. You'll have to call around and ask each practice whether it employs a vet who specializes in *exotics*, as reptiles are referred to. If you're lucky enough to have a few to choose from, you'll need to narrow the field before making a decision.

Important Considerations

First and foremost, your choice of veterinarian should be based on the doctor's knowledge and experience and on convenience of location. You need a vet who's fairly close by in case of an emergency or an ailment that requires multiple visits for treatment. Furthermore, you want a vet who has a good reputation for both skill and approachability. The final consideration is cost of care. Advanced healthcare and veterinary services can be expensive and, because important medical decisions often include financial considerations, you should compare the fees of several veterinarians.

Doing the Research

In your search for a reptile vet, chatting with other reptile owners—either in your area or on one of the many reptile-oriented forums on the Internet—is always worth your time. The reptile curator at your nearest zoo may also be able to put you in touch with a good veterinarian.

Try to find at least three practices in your area that care for exotics. Not only will this afford you the opportunity to choose

Finding a vet who specializes in exotics can be tricky. Talk to other reptile owners in your area.

the best of the three, but you'll also have a second choice to fall back on if you ever need it. Ask the vet at each practice how often he or she treats reptiles as well as whether he or she has any experience with blue-tongued skinks in particular.

Even after you've decided on a veterinarian, you should still take the opportunity to appraise both the office and the individual. Book a visit to have your new skink checked over, and make note of the pros and cons while you're there. Do you like the look of the place? Is the office staff friendly and helpful? Is the vet at ease during his or her inspection of your lizard or does he or she seem a little on edge and reluctant to touch your skink, asking you to hold it during the exam? Glance around the walls for diplomas or certificates relating to reptile care or membership in herpetological societies, and look for herpetological reference books on the shelves.

If you have your doubts about the veterinarian's knowledge of and experience with lizards, a subtle pop quiz can be helpful. Can the vet, for example, tell you what your skink should eat and at what temperatures it should be maintained? (Just don't let on that you already know the answers to these questions. Insulting your new veterinarian won't help your rapport.) If the answers to your questions are hesitant or, worse, incorrect, continue your search elsewhere.

Bear in mind that just because a vet does not have experience with your particular type of lizard doesn't automatically mean that he or she won't be able to treat it when a problem arises. The vet should have some experience with more frequently kept reptiles, such as boas, pythons, iguanas, bearded dragons, and tortoises. If your options are limited, such a vet might have just the experience you need. If all else fails, keep the phone numbers of a few suitably qualified vets handy. Your less experienced vet can call one of them for a consultation about possible treatments in a pinch.

Common Ailments and Problems

The illnesses, injuries, and diseases that occur in reptiles are too numerous to mention in this book. Some are minor and easily remedied, but many are complex and require professional treatment and even surgery. The following is a compilation of the problems that you and your pet skink are more likely to encounter during your time together.

Raw Nose (Rostral Damage)

Rostral damage is a common condition in both wild-caught and nervous captive lizards. It is caused by the reptile continually rubbing its snout against the glass surfaces of its enclosure in an attempt to reach things it can see on the other side. The rostral scale on the tip of the snout consequently erodes and starts to bleed. Although any bleeding will cease once the lizard settles down, this recurring behavior can cause scarring or permanent loss of the rostral scale as well as damage to some or all of the adjoining scales and possibly the underlying bone.

If your pet is rubbing his snout on the glass, check first that the temperature in its vivarium is not higher than it should be. Blue-tongued skinks cannot tolerate extremely high temperatures and will become agitated if

It's easy to tell a healthy snout like this one from one that's raw and bleeding from nervous rubbing.

they cannot find a cool area to retreat to. If the temperature is not to blame, try temporarily covering the exterior of the vivarium's glass areas, completely or partially, with a sheet of cardboard, paper, or plastic; this will prevent your pet from seeing objects on the other side of the glass and thereby reduce its urge to reach them. If your skink settles down and the behavior stops, permanently fix the covering on the outside of the lower part of the glass, or paint the outside of the vivarium's glass areas. As for the irritated or bleeding nose, apply a mild antiseptic and keep it clean.

Claw Problems

Blue-tongued skinks are diurnal ground-dwellers and, in the wild, will sometimes wander long distances in their search for food. As they move over varied surfaces, their claws are constantly worn down. In the confines of a vivarium, however, where such extensive movement is either restricted or unnecessary, claws can continue to grow and create discomfort. In extreme cases, one or more claws may curve beneath a foot and penetrate the flesh, causing pain and possibly leading to infection.

The obvious way to ensure that claws do not grow too long is to regularly clip them. Check your skink's feet every six to eight weeks. If you notice abnormal or excessive growth, use a pair of ordinary nail clippers to carefully trim

Make sure you clip your skink's claws regularly if its vivarium doesn't contain anything to help wear them down naturally.

them to a more respectable length. Take care to not cut too close to the toe, or you may sever the quick (the fleshy area at the base of the underside of the claw that is rich in blood vessels and is sensitive to pain).

The alternative method to trimming claws is to provide a substrate that causes the claws to wear down as the skink walks on it; one or two pieces of flat sandstone in the vivarium should work very well. Or, if you use newspaper as a substrate, you can tape a sheet of coarse sandpaper to the vivarium floor. These solutions should help keep your skink's claws nice and short naturally.

Sloughing Difficulties (Dysecdysis)

Keeping the substrate dry all of the time can cause your skink to have trouble sloughing dead skin, particularly between the toes. Dampness in the substrate helps keep the skin soft, allowing it to come off more easily. Without proper sloughing, the dead skin will remain on the lizard and gradually shrivel, which could eventually restrict the flow of blood and, in turn, result in the loss of one or more digits.

Spray the substrate beneath your skink's hides with water once or twice a day while the skink is going through

If you don't dampen the substrate to help your skink slough naturally, you'll have to manually remove dead skin occasionally.

Sloughing

Your blue-tongued skink will slough (shed its skin) periodically throughout its life to allow for growth and to replace damaged or worn skin. Juveniles may slough more frequently, but an adult will generally shed its skin four or five times a year. As the time to slough approaches, the skink's colors and markings become clouded due to the formation of a lubricating fluid between the old and new skin to aid the sloughing process. The cloudiness then disappears for a day or two, indicating that shedding is about to happen.

Unlike snakes, which typically slough their skins comparatively quickly and in one piece, lizards frequently tend to shed over several days and in bits and pieces by rubbing themselves against rough surfaces or by pulling the skin off with their mouths. Skinks frequently eat the skin as it comes off.

107

the sloughing process. Alternatively, place a container that your skink can easily enter and exit in the vivarium and fill it with damp moss or a moistened cloth.

If you choose not to moisten the substrate or provide a damp container, you'll have to manually remove the dead skin on and around your skink's toes on each foot every time your pet sloughs. Allow the skink to soak in a shallow bowl of lukewarm water for ten to fifteen minutes and then remove the shedding skin gently using tweezers.

External Parasites

Newly imported wild-caught skinks are sometimes hosts to ticks. The seller should have removed any ticks, but if he or she didn't, you'll need to remove them. Unless you keep your skink in an uncovered outdoor pen, and as long as it does not come into contact with other infested reptiles, it should then stay free of these ectoparasites for the rest of its life with you.

Ticks can cause anemia, infection, and general irritation but are easy to deal with. Remove a tick by first applying denatured alcohol or petroleum jelly to the tick's body with a cotton swab. After five or ten minutes, when the tick has suffocated, clasp its embedded head with tweezers and—so that its hooked mouthparts do not remain in the skink's body—pull it straight out in one quick movement. Apply a mild antiseptic to the area to prevent any risk of infection.

Check blue tongues for parasites such as ticks regularly if they spend a lot of time outdoors or in contact with infested reptiles.

Mites can also cause a number of problems in captive lizards, including irritation, sloughing difficulties, eye injuries, anemia, and secondary infections. You might not notice small numbers of mites, but they multiply rapidly and can survive for weeks or even months. If you ever discover mites on your skink or in the vivarium, you must start treatment immediately, especially if you have a large reptile collection.

A number of lizard-friendly sprays for eradicating mites and similar pests are available from reptile dealers, large pet stores, and veterinarians. One initial application followed by a second four weeks later is usually sufficient. Most can be used directly on your skink or its vivarium, and some are ideal for large areas—the room in which you keep your vivarium, for example. Choose one that best suits your personal circumstances and, as with any insecticide, always read the instructions carefully.

Internal Parasites

Skinks are frequently hosts to an assortment of internal parasites, including tapeworms, lungworms, roundworms, pinworms, and other nematodes. They are also susceptible to parasitic protozoan infections. Symptoms may include emaciation, bloody or watery feces, and lethargy. In some cases, you may see worms on the floor of the vivarium after your skink has defecated. Because of the complexities involved in correctly identifying such parasites and the need to determine the precise weight of any skink requiring treatment (vital for the administration of the correct dosage), it is wise to seek the advice of your veterinarian if you suspect parasites.

Your veterinarian will perform a physical examination and fecal test to confirm an infestation and to determine the type of parasite and the type and amount of medication required. He or she will then administer the medication either orally or by injection. If the vet gives you medication to take home, you must administer the *exact* amount specified or your skink could die.

Dehydration

Wrinkly skin on any part of a lizard's body—particularly around its neck—is a characteristic symptom of dehydration. A newly acquired lizard that, for example, has spent a long time in transit may suffer from such a condition. When you suspect dehydration, it is vital to consult your vet, who will probably administer fluids subcutaneously. Dehydrated animals cannot digest food properly so unless the condition is treated quickly, your skink may become emaciated.

Mouth Rot (Stomatitis)

Mouth rot is a fairly common mouth infection that affects reptiles and is characterized by a white or yellowish cheeselike matter around the gums and teeth. In acute cases, this substance can push the upper and lower labial (lip) scales apart. Mouth rot can result from an injury to the mouth, poor husbandry, stress, or a combination of these factors.

To treat the condition, remove the cheeselike matter a little at a time with a moistened cotton swab and then wash the area with a 3-percent hydrogen peroxide solution. If you catch mouth rot early, the minor infection should clear within ten to fourteen days. More advanced cases may require the attention of your vet, who may recommend antibiotics.

This is what a healthy mouth looks like—free of all signs of infection such as thick yellowish matter around the gums and teeth.

Place heating implements far enough away from your basking blue tongue to prevent thermal burns.

Thermal Burn

Blisters on the dorsal scales (those on the skink's back) are often the result of thermal burns from heaters that are too close to the skink or are unprotected. Heaters located beneath the vivarium and heat mats beneath the substrate can cause such burns on your skink's ventral surface, or underside. Make sure that your heaters are a suitable distance from the vivarium, are protected by guards, or are controlled by thermostats so that it's impossible for your pet skink to come into contact with any hot surface. Also avoid using ceramic or resin "hot rocks" (devices designed to resemble rocks that contain electronic elements), which can cause severe thermal burns.

If your pet receives an accidental burn, immediately apply a cold compress for twenty to thirty minutes to minimize further blistering. Keep the affected area clean and apply a medication made especially for the treatment of burns and other minor injuries in reptiles. If the wound does not respond to this treatment within a few days, contact your vet.

Blister Disease

Often, when a vivarium's substrate is too wet or dirty, the reptile's ventral surface becomes infected with bacteria, taking on an unnatural pinkish color and then developing reddish or brownish spots. Unchecked, these spots can continue to develop into elevated, fluid-filled blisters beneath the unfortunate reptile's scales. The blisters will burst sooner or later, leaving nasty open lesions into which further infections can gain entry.

Blister disease, also known as scale rot or vesicular dermatitis, is a fairly common problem in snakes, with their large ventral scales. It can, nevertheless, also occur in certain lizard species, particularly the larger ground-dwelling species that have more contact with the vivarium's substrate than arboreal lizards do. If your blue tongue displays the described symptoms, check that water is not overflowing when the skink enters its water bowl. In addition, make sure that the vivarium's substrate and floor are clean and free of any rotting uneaten food or fecal matter. Finally, check that the humidity in the vivarium is not too high (condensation on the inside of the glass is an indicator of high humidity).

If excessive humidity or dampness is a problem, either transfer your affected skink to a vivarium with a clean, dry, newspaper-covered floor, or remove the damp substrate and

Change your skink's substrate often to ensure healthy living conditions.

replace it with clean, dry newspaper while the blisters heal. During the healing period, either soak your skink two times a day in a watered-down (50:50) solution of chlorhexidine or povodine-iodine, or gently wash the affected scales with hydrogen peroxide every three or four days. This should take care of any infection.

In the majority of mild cases, the blisters will disappear after two sloughs, which happen more often when the lizard feels uncomfortable. Make sure that the blisters are gone, and then return your pet skink to its original vivarium or replace the temporary newspaper with fresh, dry substrate. In more severe cases—in which the blisters are more extensive or have started bursting—you must consult your veterinarian, who will clean the open lesions, apply a topical antibiotic lotion, and, if necessary, give antibiotic injections.

Wounds and Injuries

Skinks are most likely to incur wounds during combat between adult males or during mating. Superficial lacerations will generally heal quickly, but more severe wounds will need an appropriate antiseptic and daily monitoring. Newborn and sub-adult blue tongues can also cause wounds when they become very excited (usually at feeding times and especially when offered live insects). If several young skinks are housed together, they may snap at each other's toes. If a

This female suffered many small cuts when mating.

113

Reptile Respiration

In all higher animals, the general function of the respiratory system is to inhale air into the lungs so that oxygen can be absorbed into the bloodstream and to eliminate carbon dioxide, the waste gas product of living tissues, by exhaling. Reptiles are cold-blooded, or *poikilothermic*, having body temperatures that vary with those of their surroundings. Consequently, the biochemical processes that occur within their cells take place at a much slower rate compared with those of their warm-blooded counterparts, and they have less physiological need for oxygen.

So, the respiration rates of most reptiles are generally very slow. For example, large inactive species, such as crocodiles, inhale only once every few minutes. Such large reptiles are also able to hold their breath for an extended period of time without suffering the effects of hypoxia (oxygen deprivation), which, in other animals, would rapidly lead to tissue damage in the organs and brain.

skink loses a digit this way, its foot should be bathed with a reptile-friendly antiseptic.

As mentioned previously, if you or someone else picks up your skink by its tail without supporting its body, the tail can break off. The natural healing process is generally quick, but in older individuals, the wound may take longer to heal. A small part of the tail will grow back into a stump, but it will never regrow into its previous length and shape.

The tail can bleed at the site of the break, in which case you would clean the wound with an antiseptic, keep the lizard in a clean vivarium with only newspaper for flooring, and monitor its progress daily. If the wound worsens, consult your vet, who may give you a topical antibiotic.

Respiratory Problems

Infection of the airways is a common disorder that affects many captive reptiles at some point in their lives. Provided these infections are identified early, they usually respond quickly to treatment.

Correctly and hygienically maintained blue-tongued skinks are not usually susceptible to respiratory disorders. However, underfed, stressed, or newly imported specimens and those exposed to cold drafts or prolonged low temperatures may develop diseases of the respiratory tract. Other causes for respiratory problems include severe endoparasitic infestations and dirty or badly ventilated vivariums.

If your skink gets a chill, it may sneeze and begin to appear unusually sluggish. Its breathing may become rapid and labored as an infection develops, and, later, bubbly mucus may appear from the nostrils or the corners of the mouth. Simply raising the temperature of the skink's basking spot within the vivarium to between 97°F and 100°F (36°C and 38°C) for a week will, as a rule, ease the symptoms. If mucus is still present after two weeks, your vet may need to administer antibiotics.

Your healthy skink's nose and mouth should be free of the bubbly mucus that indicates a respiratory infection.

Sneezing

Every now and then, your skink may sneeze. Provided that sneezing doesn't occur repeatedly over a long period, and as long as it is not accompanied by other symptoms of illness, sneezing is just your skink's way of cleaning out its nostrils after rummaging around in the substrate.

Intestinal Infections (Enteritis)

Abnormal, watery, or blood-streaked feces; regurgitation; sudden refusal to eat; and general sluggishness can all be indicative of inflammation of the intestinal tract resulting from an infection. It goes without saying that hygiene goes a long way in preventing health problems. Always ensure that you wash your hands thoroughly before and after handling your skink. Wash well the vegetables and fruit that you offer it, and ensure that any mice, meat, and fish products come from a reliable source. In addition, if you are going to collect invertebrates from the wild, make sure they are taken from areas unaffected by insecticides and herbicides. Because enteritis comes in several forms, you should see your veterinarian as soon as possible to identify the illness and the treatment needed.

Metabolic Bone Disease (MBD)

Spinal deformities; bowed, swollen or weak limbs; and a soft, rubbery lower jaw are typical symptoms of metabolic bone disease, which may affect blue-tongued skinks of all ages. In adults, symptoms may also include quivering of the limbs and toes and, in advanced cases, convulsions. In captive blue-tongued skinks, MBD is usually a direct result of excess phosphorus in the diet, which causes the bones to weaken.

You can usually prevent bone disorders by providing your blue tongue with adequate nutrition.

MBD can also stem from an unbalanced ratio of calcium and phosphorus, inadequate dietary calcium, or insufficient exposure to UVB light. This disease is commonly known as *rickets* in juveniles and sub-adults, and as *osteomalacia* in adults. The condition can frequently be averted by providing adequate calcium and vitamin D3 supplements and increasing the skink's exposure to UVB light. In a skink already displaying the disease, such supplements will halt but not correct the deformities.

Avitaminosis B (Hypovitaminosis)

Avitaminosis B is a nutritional disorder that can develop in captive reptiles and amphibians and results from a lack of sufficient or necessary B vitamins in their diet. The form of the disease depends on which one of the B-complex components is lacking. Thiamine (B_1) deficiency affects the central nervous system, resulting in twitching limbs and possibly convulsions. A lack of riboflavin (B_2) results in paralysis of the hind limbs. You can prevent and, in most cases, cure the condition by using fresh food rather than frozen, and by regularly using a multivitamin supplement. If you are at all unsure if your pet skink's problem is a result of this deficiency, find that it isn't responding to an improved diet, or need advice on how to treat it correctly, consult your veterinarian. Don't let your lizard suffer unnecessarily.

Stress

The most obvious sign of stress in reptiles is abnormal inactivity, characterized by the animal spending most of its time hiding away and perhaps even showing a reluctance to eat, or, conversely, extreme agitation and excessive movement. Generally speaking, the blue-tongued skink is less prone to stress than many other lizard species, but even so, some can develop signs of stress in certain circumstances. Just one issue or a combination of different and often unrelated factors—including overstimulation, an unsuitable environment, and bullying—can cause stress in reptiles.

One of the more obvious reasons for a skink's stress is that it is being handled too much. Sometimes, for example,

A stressed skink will often spend most of its time in hiding.

enthusiastic and well-meaning children (and even some adults, for that matter) just don't know when to stop. They become so fascinated by and enamored with this beautiful reptile that they want to be close to it for as long as they possibly can. This is good, in theory. The more we humans "get in touch" with nature and the animals and plants with which we share this world, the more we will all benefit. However, our pets must not be forced to suffer for our interest. Limit the amount of time that you and your friends and family spend handling your skink—an hour or two a day is more than sufficient.

Also watch your lizard for signs of temperature-related agitation. Regularly check the heating and lighting equipment in your pet's vivarium to make sure that it is not producing temperatures that are too high—because of a malfunctioning thermostat, for example. Likewise, never position the vivarium in direct sunlight or next to a radiator, even for a moment; your skink can soon overheat. Other habitat-related stressors include a dirty vivarium, a too-small vivarium, and lack of a hide into which your skink can retreat completely.

To avoid stress caused by overstimulation, do not place the vivarium in a location where people are going to pass it frequently throughout the day. If this is not possible, cover the glass front with a drape (making sure, of course, that the drape doesn't come into contact with or too close to the heat source). If children can easily reach your vivarium, encourage them not to disturb the occupant by tapping on the glass. Tell them that they will be able to see far more interesting things happen if they are still and quiet.

Keeping more than one adult blue-tongued skink in the same vivarium could be stressful to one or both of them. If one remains in its hide most of the time, it could mean that the other is bullying it. Obviously, you'll need to keep two or three skinks together if you want to breed them. You should, however, keep an eye on them during this time to ensure that serious fighting does not break out between them.

Refusal to Eat

Your pet skink may suddenly refuse to eat. This is natural during breeding time, in which case there is no cause for worry, and the skink will resume feeding again once sexual activity has subsided. Outside of breeding, refusal to eat may simply indicate that the vivarium temperature is too low or that your skink is bored with its food (in which case, simply offer something different). In more serious cases, not

If you pay attention and nip problems in the bud, your skink should live a long and healthy life.

Keeping a Record

The upkeep of any animal and its habitat entails a certain amount of consistency and routine. You will find it very helpful to have some sort of record that documents such things as when your skink sloughed its skin, when it fed and what it ate, when it refused food, when its cage was cleaned, if and when it mated, the date any babies were born, and so on. You will no doubt think of other things you'd like to add, such as your skink's weight and growth rate, for example. Put together, these notes will serve as a valuable reference if problems should occur. Speaking of which, it's also important to keep a record of visits to the vet and any treatments your skink received.

The aim, whatever method is used, is to record all important events—and even some of the less important ones—that occur throughout your skink's life. These records are crucial not only in maintaining the health of your skink but also in providing your veterinarian with information necessary to make a diagnosis and treatment plan should a medical problem occur.

eating can indicate an intestinal or mouth infection that needs attention. If your lizard continues to refuse food for longer than two weeks and its condition deteriorates, consult your vet.

Consulting the Professional

I hope that this chapter will help you recognize certain problems if and when they occur. In some cases you may, by following the instructions given, be able to deal with them yourself. But you may also come across health problems that, as a beginning skink owner, you do not have the experience to deal with.

A vet has knowledge and experience that you do not have, as well as access to medications and specialized equipment. While even a brief visit to a veterinarian can be expensive, remember that consulting a veterinarian early is always better for the health of both your skink and your finances. The sicker your pet is when you take it to the vet, the more complicated and expensive its treatment will likely be compared to what it would have been had you taken it in when it first started showing symptoms of illness. If you are in any doubt at all about your pet skink's health and well-being, take it to a reptile vet.

Glossary

anal plate: The plate that covers the vent. In most lizards and snakes, it is usually distinctively larger than the other ventral scales.

brumation: A condition of torpor during extended periods of low temperatures; a state of inactivity during which the metabolic processes are greatly reduced but without actual hibernation.

cloaca: The common chamber into which the genital, urinary, and digestive canals release their contents, and which opens to the exterior through the anus or vent.

dimorphism: The morphological condition in which the male and female of a species exhibits distinct differences in color, markings, size, and/or structure.

diurnal: Active during the daylight hours.

ecdysis: The act of periodically shedding the outer layer of dead keratinous skin to permit further growth.

ectoparasite: Any parasite, such as a tick or mite, that attaches itself to the outer part of the body of its host in order to extract nourishment from blood vessels.

endoparasite: Any parasite, such as a tapeworm, that extracts nourishment from the internal parts of the body of its host.

gravid: The term used to describe the condition of a female reptile carrying eggs or young, from fertilization to the moment of birth.

hemipenis: (pl. hemipenes) The grooved copulatory organ of male lizards and snakes, paired and located within the base of the tail behind the cloaca.

herbivorous: Feeding upon grass and plant matter.

herpetology: The study of reptiles and amphibians.

invaginated: Folded inward to become sheathed.

neonate: A newborn or hatchling reptile.

omnivorous: Feeding upon both animal and vegetable matter.

ossification: The formation of bone, or the actual process of being converted to bone.

popping: The term used to describe the method of sexing juvenile reptiles involving the application of gentle pressure towards the cloaca so that the hemipenes will evert, or "pop."

seminal plug: Dried semen that adheres to the invaginated hemipenes of a male reptile, verifying that it is reproductively active.

slough: Cast off the outermost skin layer.

sub-adult: An individual lizard over twelve months of age that's sexually immature.

substrate: The surface upon or in which an animal lives, either in its natural environment, or in captivity.

vent: The hind opening located on the under surface of the body at the beginning of the tail; the external entrance/exit of the cloaca.

vermiculite: A form of expanded mica, produced for the insulation of buildings, that may also be used as an incubation medium for reptile eggs or as a substrate for baby reptiles.

vivarium: (pl. vivaria) A tank, cage, or enclosure in which living animals (generally reptiles and amphibians) are kept.

viviparous: Describing any animal in which the embryo develops within in the body of the adult female and receives its nourishment directly via some form of placenta, resulting in the eventual birth of live young.

Resources

BlueTongueSkinks.net
http://bluetongueskinks.net
Owners Zach and Holly offer a variety of skinks for sale and a comprehensive online resource for skink owners.

www.faunaclassifieds.com
This site contains numerous pages of classified advertisements from breeders, dealers, and suppliers of vivariums, lighting and heating equipment, and other skink-related necessities.

www.kingsnake.com
This is a site of great interest to new and advanced hobbyists alike, providing the very latest news on reptile expos and herpetological societies and clubs.

Pets 'N' You
717-246-1981
Red Lion, PA 17356
www.petsnyou.com
Pets 'N' You is a family-owned and -operated pet store that offers many varieties of reptile in addition to fish, small animals, and supplies.

REPTILES® Magazine
www.reptilesmagazine.com
An invaluable resource for any reptile lover, REPTILES® magazine is the ultimate guide for owners of these fascinating exotic pets.

Photo Credits

Cover photograph by fivespots (Shutterstock). robertairhart (Shutterstock): 51; arhip4: 32; aspenrock (Shutterstock): 102; John Beatty: 67, 73, 120; Doug Beckers: 89, 106; BMCL (Shutterstock): 5; Tony Bowler (Shutterstock): 26; Paul Burdett (Shutterstock): 82; Andrew Burgess (Shutterstock): 116; Denise Chan: 54; Esa/Esajaske: 45; Taniya Farooqui: 76; Isabelle Francais: 37, 39, 40, 70, 72, 74, 79, 80, 97, 99, 108; Stephanie Frey (Shutterstock): 57; Gucio_55 (Shutterstock): 83; JJ Harrison: 20, 23; Eric Isselée (Shutterstock): 105; Jakgree (Shutterstock): 7; Marina Jay (Shutterstock): 56, 112; jeffowenphotos: 35; Maria Jokinen: 111; mikakumpulainen (Shutterstock): 8; Nixx Photography (Shutterstock): 43; Siebren Kuperus: 22, 96; David Lade (Shutterstock): 114; ladyphoto (Shutterstock): 124; Paul Looyen (Shutterstock): 122-123; Timothy Craig Lubcke (Shutterstock): 48; Emily Marino: 17, 19, 33, 62, 91, 118; Rogercostamorera (Shutterstock): 100; Natalie Jean (Shutterstock): 55; Newtowngrafitti: 75; ElenaP. (Shutterstock): 28; Geoff Penaluna: 12; PetrP (Shutterstock): 98; ppl (Shutterstock): 58; Dr. Morely Read (Shutterstock): 6; rorem (Shutterstock): 4; Andrew Seike: 16, 21, 21, 87, 93, 95, 113; Miklos Schiberna: 18, 25; Mike Searson: 60; Trisha M Shears: 50; David Spencer: 66; The Reptilarium: 65; William Warby: 59; Peter Waters (Shutterstock): 10, 71, 110; ШатиллоГ.В.: 15.